A Rainbow of Rhyme

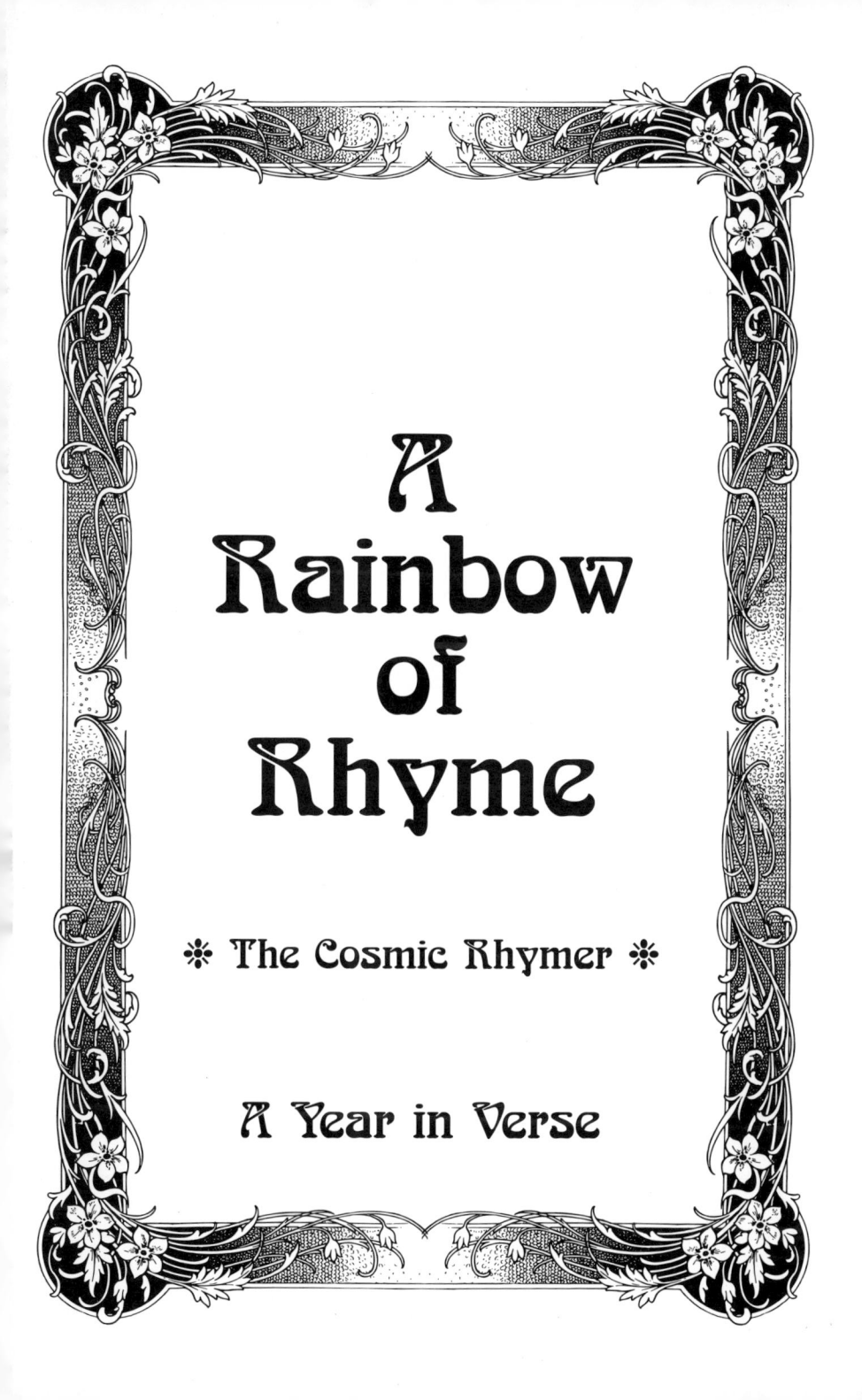

❋ The Cosmic Rhymer ❋

A Year in Verse

© Susan Armstrong-Finnerty

ISBN 978-1-0369-2278-8

Thanks to Gerd Altmann for his beautiful colour illustrations:
Gerd Altmann/geralt/pixabay.com

Cover art by:
Gordon Johnson
pixabay.com/users/gdj-1086657

and

Jochen Lengerke
pixabay.com/users/j_lengerke-8387794

Foreword

With my 60th birthday looming, I resolved to mark the milestone with a meaningful endeavour. Rhyming has long been my passion, from penning verses to brighten my husband's daily commute, to earning a spot, through my poetic flair, as a film reviewer on local radio. This love for rhyme inspired a bold challenge: to write and share a poem each day on X for a year. The result is this collection of 366 poems, capturing the rhythm of 2024, a leap year.

These poems are more than a chronicle; they are a reflection of my soul—my beliefs, joys, and values. Themes of kindness, colour therapy, self-care, astrology, crystals, nature, and playful indulgence in life's fizz and fun weave through the verses. Writing daily became a meditative anchor, sustaining me through trials like health scares, a house move, festive holidays, and quiet moments. Each rhyme imbued my days with purpose, transforming the ordinary into something profound. As a housewife in a close-knit market town, surrounded by cherished friends, I found my poems illuminated the beauty hidden in the everyday, inviting me to explore life's broader canvas.

Inspiration flowed from daily routines, beloved music, artists like Dolly Parton, and quirky celebrations like Cocktail Day. I embraced sensitive topics—illness, loss—but sidestepped politics to focus on universal truths. What began as a personal project for friends and family grew into a global conversation, with followers from a bee conservation charity to American fans delighting in my work. A poem about sheep, inexplicably, soared to over 2,000 views, while some deeply personal verses lingered in obscurity. Yet, guided by the mantra *Shine without the desire to be seen*, I persevered. A Samaritans poem, widely embraced, became a heartfelt triumph.

The journey drew local media attention, with features in a newspaper, magazine, and Radio York, alongside a warmly received talk at my local Rotary Club. With a degree in English and Drama, I continue to share rhymes on X, aspiring to perform them live one day. This collection, crafted with an open heart and a twinkle in my eye, invites you to share in the joy, resilience, and wonder of my year.

Susan Armstrong-Finnerty (The Cosmic Rhymer)
@thecosmicrhymer

I dedicate this book to:

To my husband, who has always believed in me and, even when busy, tirelessly edited my rhymes.

To Peter Bluckert, whose care and attention saved my life.

To Caroline, Emma, and Jo, my steadfast followers and cheerleaders through thick & thin.

To Steve Folland, who first gave the Cosmic Rhymer a public platform.

To Lesley Tate of the Craven Herald, for covering my story.

To Skipton Rotary, for their warm welcome.

To Aspire magazine, for excellent coverage.

To BBC Radio York and all its wonderful presenters and producers, for inviting me to share my rhymes.

To Aykut and the team at Efendy in Skipton, for their warm hospitality and peerless cuisine.

To the wonderful people of Skipton, who inspired me, encouraged me, and opened their hearts to me.

Finally, to my Dad, who also loved to rhyme, but went down the pit so that I could go to university. I love and miss you.

January

1

Today's the day you may be starting Dry January,
I wish you luck, but it's not for me.

You see, I find January a month so bleak,
One that leaves me disheartened, anxious, and weak.

Depriving myself of anything would add to my misery.
Self-care is my mantra; I'm all about glee.

So please don't view me as a problem drinker.
Au contraire, I'm a kind soul and deep thinker.

On Dry January, though, I'll take a pass,
Pour the fizz—to January joy, let's raise a glass!

2

I love Bruno Mars' *The Lazy Song*,
It captures the feeling of Today, in my bed I belong.

Those days when we've lost our mojo,
And we just can't find our get-up-and-go.

Society tells us that we must always 'do',
This song reassures us that it's enough to be you.

Alas, to stay in our bed is an opportunity so rare,
To switch the world off for a while is a very big dare.

Bruno reminds us that sometimes it's good to regress,
Now off I go to face the day, make-up on, in my red dress.

In my head, though, Bruno's song I will hum,
Outwardly in control, inside I'm giving myself permission to be a bum!

3

Today is Mind-Body Wellness Day,
Time for us to reflect how these two aspects interplay.

To bring us health and harmony,
A worthy goal for you and me.

When thoughts are bright, the body thrives,
A well of joy where vitality derives.

The mind's embrace, a healing power,
Nurturing health with every hour.

Yet when the mind is burdened or pained,
The body feels the weight, restrained.

Stress and worry, a heavy load,
Affecting the body, our spirit's abode.

So care for both, mind and shell,
Nourish thoughts, and let the body swell,

With vigour, take up Tai Chi or maybe dance,
Or on meditation, take a chance.

Find small steps that you can do,
Cherish yourself, for there's only one you.

4

My friend has suggested that when I die,
My ashes are sent in a firework into the sky.

I rather like the idea in a funny kind of way,
After all, who doesn't like a good display?

Have you thought what you want done with you?
There are lots of options of unique things to do.

Fancy being turned into a tree?
Or going out with the tide into the sea?

The way I see it, whatever way we choose,
There's no way we can really lose.

You see, I believe that when from this Earth we depart,
We'll be embraced by the Universe into its shining, loving heart.

5

January can make you feel quite blue,
So, how are we going to make it through?

Well, here's a quirky, inspired idea,
To instil in us some winter cheer.

I knew a girl who, in winter, would decorate her room,
With summer scenes, and wear sunglasses in the gloom.

She'd play *Club Tropicana*, imagine herself on the beach,
Isn't that just yearning for something out of reach?

Well, no, as all the great sages know,
Thinking about something makes it so.

So though to sunnier climes you may not be able to fly away,
In your mind and heart, you can take a summer holiday.

Now, you may think I'm off my trolley,
But my bikini's on under my coat, and I'm off to get myself a lolly!

6

In need of a boost to your self-esteem,
Purple can help you live your dream.

It's a colour that will make you feel like royalty,
Providing an air of mystery for you and me.

Luxury can be had by donning this hue;
When you wear purple you're wise and your words ring true.

Creativity on the wearer it can bestow,
And a sense of peace to help you go with the flow.

Associated with dignity and the divine,
Put purple in your life, and you will shine.

7

The poem *Invictus*, written by William Ernest Henley,
Is a very special work to me,

Beloved also by Nelson Mandela,
Whom I'm sure you'd agree was quite a fella.

It tells of the unconquered nature of the soul,
Tempered in life's furnace, taking its toll.

The message it bears shines bright and true,
In life, many bad things may happen to you.

But cling tight to the strong spirit within,
Then, my friend, you'll be a warrior and win, win, win.

8

Some monks make beautiful works of art from sand,
When they are done, they destroy them with their own hand.

Today, I dismantled Christmas in our nest,
It made me a little sad 'cause Christmas is the time I love the best.

Though if it were Christmas throughout the year,
We'd miss out on the joy of its transient cheer.

Life, too, should be approached this way;
Who knows how long on this Earth is our stay?

So let's relish the moments and people and love them so,
Then be prepared to say thanks and let it all go.

9

AI is dominating the news,
Does it scare you, or amuse,

With all the things it can do?
For it can do a lot, that's true.

From art to health, it has a role:
Improving lives; reaching our goal.

It translates chats with foreign friends,
Ensuring our bond never ends.

In writing a novel, you can now ace,
You can even make a friend in the digital space.

It's not perfect though, in life when you're facing a trial,
All you need is a genuine human smile.

And though some days your duties you may like to shirk,
AI may one day put you out of work.

So with AI, let's stop and think,
Let's take control now, for of historic change, we are on the brink.

10

In a world where conformity reigns supreme,
Standing out may seem like a distant dream.

But listen closely, let me make it clear,
Your idiosyncrasies you should hold dear.

Embrace the quirks that set you apart,
Let your individuality be your art,

For in a tapestry of monotone hues,
your vibrant colours refuse to lose.

You need not fit within a tight confine,
Let your brilliance sparkle and shine.

Dare to be different, let your spirit unfurl,
For it's in authenticity you'll find your pearl.

So don't worry if you're not like the rest,
Being yourself is what truly is best.

In a world that demands boring conformity.
It's unique souls that shine eternally.

11

In ancient Norse lore time,
Thursday birthed from powers divine.

Thor, with hammer strong and bold,
With awe and reverence his tale is told.

With thunder roars and lightning bright,
He waged his battles; fears took flight.

A day to honour his strength and grace,
Thursday's a time to claim our hero's place.

Where in your world could you be like Thor,
Making your body strong by doing more?

Or finally showing that loser the door—
Take up your symbolic Hammer, let's show this Thursday what for.

12
I once had to write a review,
Of the film *Frozen*, O! what a lovely thing to do,

I can hear you cry, but wait until you've heard what I've got to say,
I'm the one person in the world who didn't enjoy it in any way.

The songs, bar one, were forgettable, though the visuals bold,
The characters and their situations left me cold.

The ice queen's struggles, her internal strife:
The score and animation did not bring them to life.

As the credits rolled and the lights did glow,
I couldn't shake off the feeling of woe.

A chill in the air, a frosty blow,
At the end of it all, I just wanted to *Let it Go.*

13
Today I was in the supermarket aisle,
Instead of dashing, I lingered a while.

Taking time to contemplate,
The variety of foods on offer to put on our plate.

The array of foods is so fine,
Here's a thought, though, they are also divine.

In Greece, honey was considered a food fit for a god,
Whilst in Egypt, the pomegranate was revered, a fact that might seem odd.

For the Aztecs, a sacred food was corn,
And ancient Christians with the fish symbol their homes would adorn.

As the climate changes and we let food perish,
It's time that our food we began cherish.

14

In Japan is a special form of art,
That might help you if you feel your life or self's falling apart.

It's called *Kintsugi* and uses broken pottery.
What could be its message for you and me?

When a pot breaks, perhaps because it's old,
The broken parts are mended with lacquer and gold.

No pretending that it was never broken, or always right,
The imperfect places they highlight.

What is the message that we could take away,
From this practice to help us in our darkest day?

This: when we break as people, we create a space,
For light to enter and help us restore our place.

Perfection in life should not be our goal,
As there's beauty in brokenness; it's good for our soul.

15

This is the day we are told that is called Blue Monday,
A day when depression and despair hold sway.

The middle of January; money is tight,
The weather is awful; nothing seems right.

But did you know this is Brew Monday too?
The Samaritans strategy for me and you.

It's to call a friend and have a coffee and a chat,
Lifting your mood can be as simple as that.

What if you don't have a friend and feel alone?
Call the Samaritans: kindness is there at the end of a phone.

16

Feeling like your life's a folly?
Well take heart and be more Dolly!

For Dolly Parton has much to say,
About life that can help smooth our way.

Storms make trees take deeper roots,
Helps us weather bad times and life's disputes.

You'll never do a whole lot unless you're brave enough to try,
Will pick us up when our motivation has said Bye-bye.

The way I see it, if you want a rainbow, you've got to put up with the rain,
Lets us know brighter times will arrive after our pain.

Finally, *The magic is inside you, there ain't no crystal ball,*
Picks us up off the ground and makes us stand tall.

So thank you, Dolly, for your words so fine,
You've beauty within and you help our world shine.

17

In winter's grasp, when skies are grey,
We yearn for signs to light our way.

In nature's script, a resilient theme,
The first signs of spring, a hopeful dream.

Beneath the snow, where secrets lie,
A symphony stirs, a soft reply.

Tiny shoots emerge, breaking the earth,
A metaphor for our own rebirth.

As crocuses peek, heads held high,
In our own hearts, a whispered sigh.

A warmth that spreads, a gentle breeze,
The thaw of troubles, put at ease.

Budding branches, a canvas bright,
Painting hope in the morning light.

Birds sing a melody sweet,
Echoing the joy our hearts repeat.

Nature's chorus, a song of revival,
A reflection of our own survival.

In life's garden, we too shall find,
The shoots of hope within the mind.

Petals opening, resilience shown,
A testament to strength we've known.

So, let us seek the signs of spring,
In every moment, let hope sing.

Through trials faced, we made it through our pain,
Like spring's glory, we too will rise again.

18
Today, something I'd been looking forward to,
At the last minute, fell through.

I had a choice; I claim that in life I'm positive.
Could I rise to that claim and forgive,

The folks who had messed with my day?
Well, I didn't do it straight away.

Then I came across this quote,
Some words that Martin Luther King Jr. wrote:

We must accept finite disappointment, but never lose infinite hope,
I must admit it helped me cope.

I was gentle with myself for experiencing a blow,
But onwards and upwards; I'm back fighting; and here I go.

19
I love a thesaurus; it's a wonderful thing.
It can lift my rhymes from the mundane and help my poetry sing.

I am a wordsmith so keen,
A thesaurus ensures I can say what I mean.

Eloquent expressions, a vivid array,
Coloured by the thesaurus in a linguistic ballet.

Precision and flair, expressing my highs and lows,
With the help of its magic, my poetry flows.

Oh, the thesaurus, a loyal comrade,
It leaves me rejoicing instead of just glad.

So here's to the thesaurus, a companion true,
Unveiling possibilities, a linguistic breakthrough.

In the dance of words, it takes the lead,
The loyalist of friends in the hour of every writer's need.

20

If it's your birthday today, you're an Aquarian,
Your intellect and creativity win you many a fan.

You like to solve problems and are not a complainer,
For good causes, you are a campaigner.

Independent and assertive,
You push boundaries and are progressive.

Sharing your birthday with Oprah Winfrey and Justin Timberlake,
With a stubborn streak, once made up, your mind you will not unmake.

The symbol for your sign is the Water Carrier,
You have a need to innovate and won't accept any barrier.

To progress, you will swim against the tide,
A little eccentric, you wear your originality with pride.

So enjoy your birthday, dear lover of the human race,
For at being one of a kind, you simply ace.

21

I am a fan of astrology,
And two planets bring joy to me.

For me, Jupiter and Venus are the best;
I'm quite indifferent to the rest.

In astrology, Jupiter brings wealth,
And restores your body to optimum health,

Bringing miracles and fortune and all that's good.
Of course, I love Jupiter; anyone would.

Venus, too, for me is a planet of note,
Governing attraction and pleasure; it floats my boat.

Imagine my shock when I made the discovery,
That these two planets are quite horrible in reality.

The pressure on Venus would crush your head;
It's so hot there it can melt lead.

Jupiter, by contrast, is amazingly cold;
Time goes faster there, so in a flash, you are old.

I think it's best if on these startling facts I don't dwell,
I prefer the romantic view of my planets where all is love and all is well.

22

Van Gogh said, *If you love nature, you'll find beauty everywhere*,
I agree, even if, one day, your life is filled with woe and care,

A spider's web can be a wondrous sight,
Illuminating your world with a little light.

The other day I saw an ice pattern on a car,
It shimmered like a magical star.

I was just off to the shops to do my stuff.
That little bit of beauty, though, was enough,

To take me out of my daily grind,
Putting loftier ideas in my mind.

So when you just want to look down, look around,
For in a moment, a lovelier world can be found.

23

In the attic of my mind, where memories reside,
A child's laughter echoes, a joy I can't hide.

Nurturing the spirit, like a garden to sow,
I rediscover the wonders of the long ago.

With glitter on lots of things I used to make,
Weaving scarves with a loom, an age would take.

On my Etch a Sketch, I would produce fantastic works of art,
Making up dances to the latest hits on the chart.

Now older, my inner child is still what you can see,
When I send you a card with additions by me.

The child within, with eyes wide and bright,
Still dances every morning, making my adult world right.

You see, our child waits within for us to bring them joy
So off you go, find that joy, that laughter no care can destroy.

24

In the realm of tasks, where time slips away,
Procrastination lurks, tempting us to delay.

A dance with excuses, a waltz with the clock;
Yet the remedy lies in a simple, bold talk.

Just do it, the mantra to declare,
Break free from the chains, breathe in the fresh air.

No more stalling, no more delay,
Take that first step, on today, National Just Do It Day.

The list may be daunting, the mountain high;
But conquer we shall, reaching for the sky.

No more Tomorrow, no more Not Now.
Seize the moment and embrace the power of now.

Procrastination is a phantom, a trick of the mind;
With determination, its grip you'll unwind.

Turn the tide and let motivation ignite;
Face the challenge and embrace the fight.

Now rally your courage and summon your grit.
Defeat procrastination; don't let it sit.

In the arena of action, let triumph be writ,
For in just doing it, you'll be your own greatest hit.

25

The weather was grim, my head was bowed down,
I found a million reasons to make me frown.

I hated the wind and I hated the rain.
It all seemed hopeless, all seemed pain.

Then, a little tune came to me,
From the musical about a brave little girl, Annie.

The tune assured me that *The sun'll come out tomorrow.*
Could it be true, might it appear and chase away my sorrow?

As I hummed the song, I could feel hope arise,
Yes, surely tomorrow there'll be blue skies.

Till then, I'll find ways to get me through,
Little treats and nice things I can do,

To keep the sun within me burning bright.
For in the darkest of days, we must keep searching for the light.

26

What does a bed mean to you?
A place to relax or tasks to pursue?

Snuggling up or scrolling on your phone,
A chance to be together or luxuriate in being alone.

To Tracey Emin, it was a work of art,
For some, a bed's a place to refresh their heart.

In bed, some people battle every night,
With insomnia or dreams that give fright.

Not just a piece of furniture, a bed is much more,
Have a think and decide what yours is for.

Then create your haven, don't hesitate,
Becoming your own favourite bedmate.

27

Saturday: when we are finally free,
Named after Saturn, the symbol of discipline in astrology.

In this realm, Saturn signifies order and hard work every day,
Yet on Saturday, we should cast it away.

Saturn, stern ruler of effort and toil,
Will try his hardest our relaxation to foil.

But as Saturday dawns, we yearn for release,
To shed the constraints and find inner peace.

Responsibility's burden, a weight to bear,
On weekdays it lingers, a constant affair.

Yet as Saturday beckons, a respite longed for,
It's time to show Saturn the door.

Work and duty: let them rest a while;
On this day, let laughter beguile.

Remembering the irony, let the good times roll,
Saturday's a time to replenish heart, body, and soul.

28

I woke up today, our hot water was cold,
So my hair remained tangled, a sight to behold.

I lamented: our boiler was on the blink,
I got grumpy, then I started to think.

To enjoy water at all means I'm a lucky gal,
For some must walk miles to a well.

One in ten, a staggering plight,
With water scarce, far from sight.

Walking miles through unforgiving heat,
Aching backs and blistered feet.

Water is more than just a need,
It's hope, it's health, it's how we feed.

So let my hair remain tangled, perfection I won't chase,
Just hope for a clean abundant water for all of the human race.

29

If you were a flower, what kind would you be?
Maybe you don't want to be a flower, but an imposing oak tree.

For me, a Dahlia would suit fine,
Bold and colourful, standing proud, not toeing the line.

Perhaps you'd prefer to be a flower in the wild,
Non-conformist, free to express your inner child.

The exotic orchid might appeal to you,
Expressing your sexiness, a tool to woo.

If today you are thinking of yourself more as a weed,
Choose again, in your mind, a more positive bloom—plant the seed.

30

In the realm of friendship, oh what a treasure,
Laughs and secrets we always measure.

Through thick and thin, come rain or shine,
Together we stand, a duo divine.

Like two peas in a pod, we stick like glue,
Sharing the sunny times and those that are blue.

We're partners in crime, a dynamic pair,
With inside jokes that we love to share.

When life gets tough, you're my lifeline,
With you by my side, everything's just fine.

You're the custard to my jelly,
Sharing deep thoughts and what we love to watch on the telly.

Through silly antics and crazy schemes,
We conquer the world, or so it seems.

With you, my friend, the laughter never ends,
Any differences our bond transcends.

So here's to us, the ultimate team,
In the friendship game, we reign supreme.

31

I'd like to offer you a job in PR.
Your role would be to make yourself the Star.

Though you may feel that you'll never win,
Because of past mistakes, but these you can spin,

Into triumphs and challenges you've met on your path.
With your amusing tales, you'll make others laugh.

Believe in yourself, and others will too.
Let your passion and drive guide you through.

Perhaps you'd feel there's nothing starry about you.
Hold that thought and contemplate all you do.

You're a brilliant partner, colleague, friend.
You are caring and have patience without end.

If you think the way you look ain't so grand,
Be assured: your beauty is unique; for yourself, take a stand.

Be your own PR agent, shine with confidence bright.
You are a Star, and to be applauded. You have that right.

February

1

A little secret I'd like to share:
I'm a polite, caring, lady who likes to swear.

You see, I think there are situations in life that we go through,
When only an expletive will do!

Yes, though it's not my intention to invoke shocks,
Sometimes it's clear, people are talking b***ocks.

When with a curve ball we are hit,
Surely we're allowed to declare *That was s**t?*

I always feel better, never worse,
If I allow myself a little curse.

Whenever I'm feeling sorry for me,
I let it all go with an expressive profanity.

Luckily now, we have the odd abbreviation,
If we are worried about our reputation.

This means that, if in public, we can try our luck,
Sparing blushes by declaring, WTAF.

I think I'll end my rhyme for today,
Because, to be frank, I CBA!

2

In the morning light, with eyes aglow,
Comes bounding forth, our furry friend, to show,

The boundless joy that pets impart,
And a love so pure, it warms the heart.

With wagging tails and gentle purrs,
They chase away our daily blurs.

Through the lands of mischief, they often roam,
Yet, in our hearts, they find a home.

They chase their tails with gleeful delight,
Or chew our slippers through the night.

And yet we never see red,
Even when they puke on our freshly-made bed.

Though frustrations may briefly sting,
Love for our pets forever will cling.

A faithful companion, through triumph and cries,
We always find acceptance in their eyes.

Their love unwavering, steadfast, and true,
A treasure beyond measure, through and through.

From playful romps to cosy snuggles,
Their presence soothes, like warm bath bubbles.

In their company worries fade away,
As they teach us to live, laugh and play.

So let's cherish our wonderful furry friends,
Whose love and joy know no ends.

For in their japes we find the key,
To a life filled with fun and glee.

3

Does your life ever feel like it's *Groundhog Day*,
Doing the same old things in the same old way?

Well, here's a little tip for you,
A thought to help you appreciate your life anew:

Imagine that this was the last time you could do that thing,
Like washing up, which never makes your heart sing.

What if the water dried up and didn't flow,
To clean your dishes. Where would you go?

Each week you have to do a big shop,
Now the shelves are empty—planning your fancy meals has to stop.

That call you make out of duty once a week,
The lines are down—now it's connection that you seek.

If we use our imagination, we can appreciate,
Our lives filled with small things are miraculous and great.

4

The phoenix, a symbol in ancient mythology,
Holds an important lesson today for you and me.

By the flames, it was destroyed,
But it rose again from the void.

In our lives, we may face the fire—
Illness, adversity, or the loss of our heart's desire.

Feeling bereft and scared, like we can't cope,
Contemplating the phoenix can give us hope.

Darkest days test our mettle and prove our worth:
The flames won't destroy us; we will get our magnificent rebirth.

5

When you hear the word *nickname*, how do you feel?
Does it make you smile, or slightly reel?

In our lives we have probably all had a few,
Some in our hearts will still like glue.

At school, I had a couple that were quite vile.
Now grown, I'm pleased to say, all of mine make me smile.

I'm proud to be christened *The Bargain Queen*.
And the name Liz (after Liz Taylor) is clearly not mean.

Mystic Violet after my hair colour seems to fit,
All my nicknames now with me are a hit.

In my heart, though, I'll always carry a little hurt,
Caused by the ones aimed at me like dirt.

If any nicknames have affected you so,
Be kind to yourself and let them go.

Christen yourself with ones that are positive,
Then a happier life you will live.

So whether you're *Cuddles* or *Snuggle bum*,
Claim the good ones—time to be your own best chum.

6

In life's grand tapestry, a hue so bold,
Radiating warmth:shimmering gold.

It's more than a colour, it's a beacon, you see,
Uplifting the spirit and setting the soul free.

When days feel heavy, burdened with strife,
Gold whispers of promise, igniting new life.

It dances with sunlight, painting the sky,
Filling each moment with hope flying high.

Embrace optimism with it's luminous sheen,
Look to the future and forget what's been.

With gold as your guide, the darkness recedes,
Strength and energy bloom; abundant gold fulfils your needs.

So embrace this hue, let its power unfold,
For with gold in your life, you'll never feel old.

With gold in your life you'll find your true worth,
Claiming your role as a King or Queen of the Earth.

7

I'm not a Pagan, but in those beliefs I find much good,
Lessons for life and how we should,

Have reverence deep for earth and sky,
And heed nature's suffering cry.

In modern days, their wisdom gleams,
A beacon bright in troubled streams.

In cycles spun, they honour Gaia's grace,
Embracing life in every place.

As time moves on throughout the year,
They celebrate with fire, driving away the fear.

In their ways, we find the key,
To nurture our planet home, our destiny.

To view ourselves as part of all,
To heed the Earth's enduring call.

With Pagan lore, we can restore,
The harmony we seek once more.

8

Fairytales are criticised today, in lots of ways.
When I was little, they helped me through my darkest days.

A particular favourite was Snow White,
Which gave me hope of a future so bright.

Before you judge, and give a wince,
It had nothing to do with a handsome prince,

Rescuing me and making life good;
But survival through a scary wood,

That I struggled to find my way through.
In the end, I rescued myself, as we all should do.

Cinderella, too, touched my heart.
Again, the Prince played a minor part.

No, the message to me was clear:
Stay true to yourself and hold your values dear,

Then the cruelness of others over you will hold no sway,
You will get your triumphant day.

So before these tales of old we criticise,
Remember the messages they contain, so wise.

9

In Brazil's heart, where rhythms ignite,
Lies a carnival—a dazzling sight.

A fiesta of colours, a jubilant spree;
The world's grandest party for all to see.

With samba's sway, the streets come alive,
In every step spirits thrive.

Dancers dressed in feathers and lace,
Moving as one, in a rhythmic embrace.

Costumes ablaze with vibrant hues,
The magic of Carnival will uplift and amuse.

Sip on caipirinhas, refreshing and cool,
In the carnival heat, they're the perfect fuel.

So let's throw a bash, in February's grey,
A Brazilian carnival to chase the blues away.

With costumes, music, dance, and cheer,
Let's make our own carnival atmosphere!

10

Losar Sang means Happy New Year in Tibetan.
Today begins the Year of the Dragon.

In the snowy peaks where prayer flags fly,
Tibetan New Year paints the sky.

With drums and chants, the mountains resound,
As the Year of the Dragon is crowned.

Butter lamps flicker; offerings are made,
To honour ancestors, in reverence paid.

Dancing in circles, beneath the moon's gleam,
Welcoming prosperity and freedom's dream.

With colourful masks and swirling dance,
Blessings bestowed, a sacred trance.

We can embrace this ritual too,
Letting the new moon bless me and you.

Whether you're a Pig, Horse or Snake,
With this celebration, a fresh path you can take.

So let Losar Song enrich our day,
And illuminate our lifelong way.

11

Have you ever contemplated the wonder of the sky,
On a sunny day, dreaming a dream as the clouds roll by?

Or gazing up on a starry night,
Its vast glory making your world seem right?

Sometimes a rainbow appears and brings us joy,
A piece of magic, our spirits to buoy.

Even when the sky is grey,
A soaring bird may make our day.

So come rain, come shine, if given the chance,
Look up and appreciate this amazing expanse.

12
If you had your own coat of arms,
How would it show the world your charms?

Maybe a phoenix would make sense,
To symbolise your resilience.

To demonstrate your strength, perhaps an oak tree,
Or a lion to show courage in the face of adversity.

Your kindness could be shown with an outstretched hand,
A jester's hat for your humour surely would be grand.

Why not make yourself a coat of arms today?
You'll have fun and learn to value yourself along the way.

13
We live in a world of technology,
And sometimes I wonder how nice it would be:

If every day when I woke,
These words I could hear spoke:

Power On and *Fully Charged*, then off I'd go,
Immediately functioning and in my flow.

Alas! It takes much more,
To get me going and out the door.

I need a coffee and a shower to feel right,
Or you may see a red warning light,

Signalling that my battery is low;
My energy is gone; I'm on a go slow.

Long live my dream of just being able to be plugged in,
Sadly, it takes effort in this life to win!

14

Valentine's Day: no card—you're feeling blue,
Tonight's dinner will be microwaved, and for one—not a cosy meal for two.

My friend, I urge you, don't fall for the advertiser's hype,
That you are nothing in this world until you find your type.

You see, loving comes in many forms, all special in their way,
So remember who you love and who loves you today.

Go buy yourself a tasty meal, or another indulgent treat,
Remember: you don't need anybody else to feel worthy and complete.

Then, tonight, it's yourself you will have wined and dined,
Instead of spending a day when you whined and pined.

Take care of you, then in-love with yourself you'll fall,
For as Whitney sang, *Learning to love yourself is the greatest love of all.*

15

Buddha once ate meat, even though he was a vegetarian,
Though you might not approve, he was a special kind of man.

Kindness was so important to him,
He'd rather go against his principles than leave others feeling grim.

So when invited to a meal, off he went,
Blessing the family and the hospitality so well meant.

He ate pork and left his hosts feeling bright,
The lesson for us, when endeavouring to do right:

Let kindness be your overriding principle,
Put that at the heart, for it will always fit the bill.

16

In February's final days, when skies seem grey,
Random kindness comes to light our way.

In the midst of chill, warmth can be felt,
And with simple acts, our hearts can melt.

No grand gesture needed; just the will to do a little thing,
That will make another's heart sing.

Like anonymously bringing in your neighbour's bin,
The smallest act for someone can feel like a big win.

Though today you may have a million things to do,
Let someone go ahead of you in the queue.

Each of these tiny sparks of generosity,
Illuminate our path, so I becomes we.

As we look forward to winter finally taking flight,
Random Acts of Kindness will make the world a little more bright.

17

Some days you just have to get by,
Things don't come together, no matter how you try.

And though at life you usually ace,
Today's a day you just can't face.

Forgive yourself, because no two days are the same;
You can't always be at the top of your game.

Seek out one thing that will help you cope:
A caring friend, or an uplifting film to give you hope,

That you can regain your mojo and find your way,
For tomorrow truly is another day!

18
Bacchus is a god of fun and play,
So let's say *Cheers!* to him on National Drink Wine Day.

With wine, there's health in every pour,
Know the benefits, and it's not just the taste you'll adore!

Heart health is wine's great gift, with antioxidants in its blend,
It keeps your ticker ticking—a longevity trend!

Resveratrol, a magic word, found in the grape's red skin:
It fights off ageing, it's like a sip of youth within!

But don't go wild, for moderation is the key,
Too much of a good thing's not wise for you or me.

So raise your glass, let's have a toast, to this quirky wine-filled event,
With joy and health in every sip, some might argue wine was Heaven-sent.

19
Today it's time to wish happy birthday to those who share the Pisces sign,
They are lovely folk who are imbued with the divine.

Pisces is the first sign of spring, a sense of hope it imparts;
Pisceans are gentle souls with empathetic hearts.

Symbolized by fishes, swimming in celestial streams;
Trustworthy and loyal—their friendship gleams.

Deep down they are sensitive, but to hound them pessimism tries.
By using their imagination, they escape to the skies.

With Justin Bieber and Rebel Wilson in their ranks,
For their artistry and creativity to all Pisceans we give thanks.

20

Life is a journey, and it's hard.
It's not a surprise that many of us get scarred.

That's why I admire people of a certain age:
They've made it through each thorny stage.

Now, still they battle on through loss and pain,
Surviving one more day, wisdom to gain.

So when we see the elderly, let us not turn away,
For they deserve admiration and respect, every day.

They are heroes for still being here;
And not giving in to loneliness, despair or fear.

Like everyone, they yearn to be seen,
For all that they are and all that they've been.

From them we have so much to learn.
Remember: one day, at being old, you'll have your turn.

21

In strange places, where paths entwine,
A friend awaits a gem to find.

Amidst the whirl of life's daily grind,
Opportunities for friendship you can find.

Yet most of us spend our time alone,
Tethered to the screen of our phone.

Away from gadgets, in a USB-free zone,
Conversations flow and seeds are sown.

With open hearts and ears to lend,
A stranger can become a friend.

But if a chat feels off, or seems askew,
Assert yourself and bid Adieu.

For our daily encounters should delight,
Nourishing our souls and keeping our spirits bright.

Embrace the chance in each meeting,
Even if it's random or fleeting.

For strangers are friends in the making,
Just open your heart: friendship is there for the taking.

22

Though my school days are now lost in the mists of time,
I'd like to dedicate this little rhyme,

To the teachers who taught me more than how to read and write;
Those who made an insecure girl's world at moments seem right.

There was Mrs. Cat who cast me in a starring role,
So affirming for my quite lost soul.

And Mr. Linney who made maths seem okay,
When I'd failed at it twice and lost my way.

Finally, Mr. Remmington was a gent amongst men,
An English teacher who bestowed on me a love of the pen.

So thank you, teachers, I carry your gifts in my heart,
You were heroes, for it was not just facts, but belief, you did impart.

23

Philip Treacy, the milliner, is the master of the hat.
He said, *Hats are radical; only people who wear hats understand that.*

But, today, a hat is an item of clothing that so few people choose,
Except when going to a do, or Ascot for the booze.

It's such a shame, as hats can make you feel a certain way,
Feeling a little French? Why not go for a beret?

Maybe today you want a little mystery?
A tilted trilby would fit the job; just a little of your face we'd see.

Yearning to escape the crowds and head for a wide open plain?
Why not wear cowboy hat? Such freedom you would gain.

Throw caution to the wind. Go on! Be brave!
Try wearing a hat today—think of the hair gel that you'll save!

24

In February's sky, the full moon gleams,
Known as the *Bone Moon* in native dreams.

Where once they gnawed on bone and marrow,
Surviving during the season fallow.

In Asian tales, the *Budding Moon* is its name,
Symbolizing new starts, nurturing a flicker into a flame.

When Lunar New Year celebrations ignite,
Hope blossoms anew under its guiding light.

As we gaze upon this lunar sight,
We applaud our resilience, our souls' might.

Through our own winters, we did preserve,
Now the promise of spring draws near.

So let us embrace this full moon's glow,
With hearts uplifted, we welcome the show.

25

I love to be by the sea,
When there, I can just be.

I don't have to stress or strive;
It's enough to be alive.

As I watch the tide ebb and flow,
Any hurt or pain, I let it go.

The sea gives me a sense of infinity;
I feel boundless, so much more than me.

As I gaze upon this vista vast,
I'm in the present, no care of future or of past.

In touch with nature and the divine,
I believe that other worlds can be mine.

So when I die, please don't cry or bawl;
Give me to the sea, then I'll be one with all.

26

We all need a toolkit for life,
To help us through our trouble and strife.

In mine is my favourite disco track,
It makes my world sparkle when all seems black.

Oh, and what's this? It's a big cream bun,
That will always give me a sense of fun.

Now here's an episode of my favourite soap,
With most of life's ills it will help me cope.

Perhaps start to assemble your toolkit today,
So it's ready when you feel you have lost your way.

Does it contain a kitty cuddle,
To ground you when your head's in a muddle?

Or perhaps some fresh air and a run,
To lift your spirits when you feel done?

Put whatever gives you pleasure in your toolkit,
Then to face life's battles, you'll be fighting fit.

27

There was a glam girl from Skipton town,
Who, approaching 60, felt quite down.

So she picked up her pen,
Rhymed again and again;

Now she's wearing the CosmicRhymer crown!

28
A Sheep Rhyme from Sheep Town—Skipton

In fields of green where daisies peek,
Lives a creature known as the sheep.

With woolly coats, they frolic and play,
Bleating merrily, come what may.

As springtime blooms, they're the first to show,
A fluffy sign that winter's let go.

Alas, as a cutlet, they'll meet their fate,
Here, though, is something to contemplate.

From sweaters warm to cosy socks,
They are worth so much more than lifeless chops.

Through rain or shine, they stand serene,
Enduring all, a steadfast scene.

Lessons aplenty from these friends,
Their patience and resilience never ends.

So let's admire their simple grace,
In every bleat, a lesson to embrace.

For in the life of the humble sheep,
There's wisdom profound, for us to keep.

29

Today you've been given an extra 24 hours,
So you can stop and smell the flowers.

Or perhaps propose to your soul mate?
Remember this day is yours to create.

So grab the day by the balls,
Don't spend it making routine calls.

Do something that will nurture your spirit within,
At last: a battle with time that you can win.

Whatever you do today, be it shallow or deep,
Cherish this time, then tomorrow, into spring, you will leap.

March

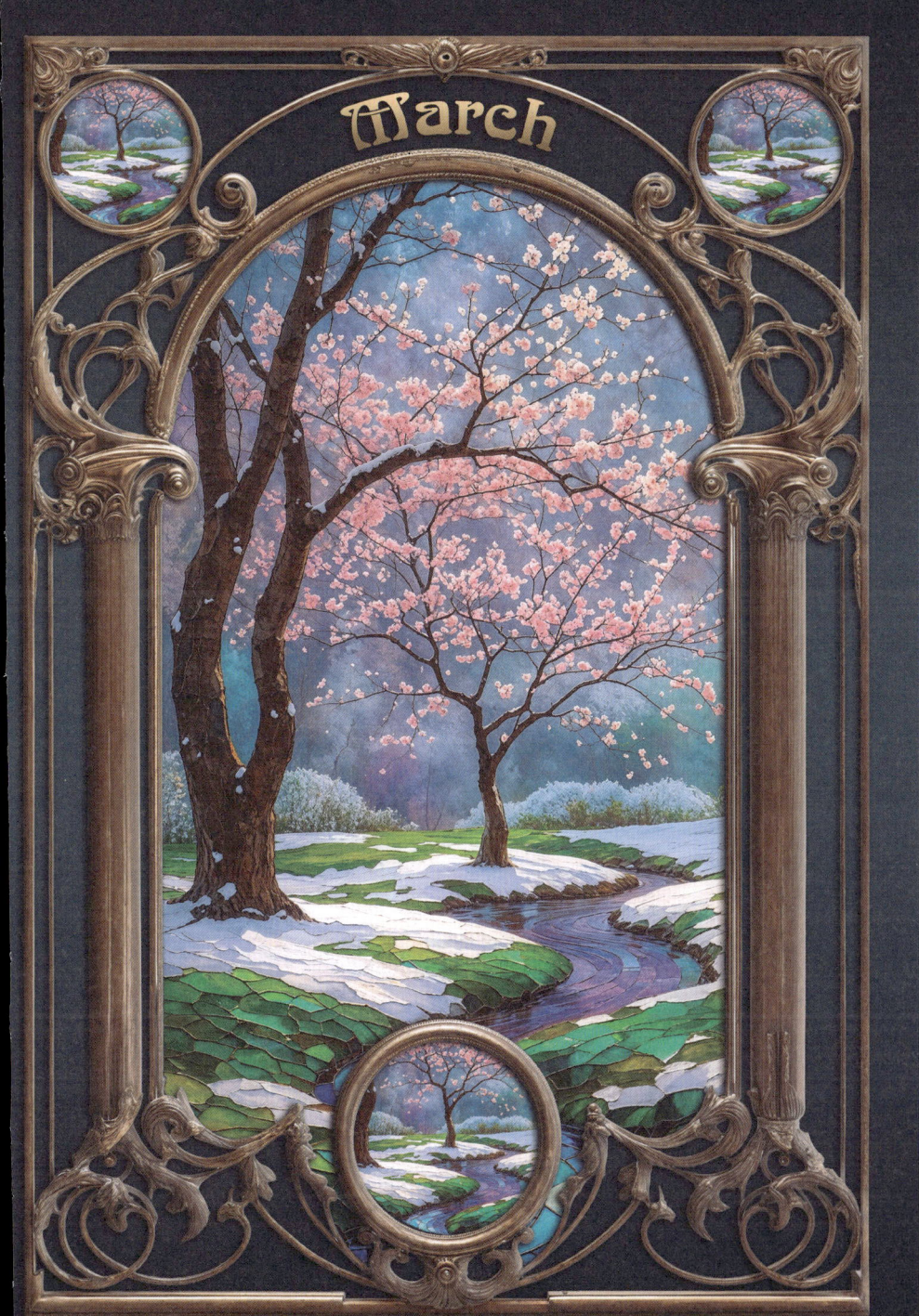

1

As winter's grip begins to fade away,
And springtime heralds a brand new day,

Nature's New Year dawns with light and cheer,
A time for fresh starts, so crystal clear.

The first day of spring, a gift for you,
To add extra oomph to all you do.

In winter it's hard to pursue your goal;
Spring's energy and rhythm can refresh your soul.

It's the time to have a chance to renew,
Resolutions, seeing dreams blossom, strong and true.

So let the first day of spring be your cue,
To seize the moment, and boldly pursue,

The paths that lead to your heart's desire,
As Nature's New Year fuels your inner fire.

2

In the realm of hues, there's a shade serene:
Silver—a whisper; a tranquil scene.

Like the lining of clouds, it softly gleams,
In its gentle embrace, we find our dreams.

Feminine grace it embodies with pride,
Linked to the moon, where mysteries hide.

Under silver's soft gentle glow,
We find calm in its tranquil flow.

In times of change, it's our guiding light,
Reflecting our journey, clear and bright.

Amidst life's twists, it shows us a way,
To navigate forward, come what may.

Glamorous allure it effortlessly brings;
Of elegance and charm it softly sings.

So let's embrace this colour so fine:
A spiritual mirror that reflects the divine.

3

Numerology explains that numbers are important in our lives.
And that it is from numbers that our luck derives.

I am not sure that I believe that claim,
But I have numbers that I'm fond of all the same.

Like many folks, I adore the number seven,
When I encounter it, I always view it as a sign from Heaven.

I'm also keen on the number four,
And wouldn't argue if it graced my front door.

Yet in some cultures, four is viewed with disdain,
Sounding like death, a haunting refrain.

Of course, the number thirteen always brings fear,
Superstitions abounding as the date draws near.

However, though we may respect numbers and their power,
Remember to always be the number one hero of your hour.

4

If Monday leaves you feeling *bleugh* or bleak,
Cheer up, friend, it's National Pie Week!

Indulge yourself with your favourite flavour,
The one that you truly love to savour.

It's no longer just a pie and a pint for lunch,
The pie has gone posh—have a gastro pie for brunch.

There are so many varieties to try,
Venison and port is a thing, not just pie in the sky.

In North Yorkshire, it's the Pork Pie that is most celebrated,
Whose is the best is keenly debated.

Also, should a pie have a top AND bottom crust?
Well, for me, it should—that pie rule is a must.

Seeking to become the apple of someone's eye?
Then my advice is to take them out for a pie.

Shepherd's, or Clanger, or a Cumberland Rum Nicky,
There's a pie just for you, no matter how picky.

Pies are perfect for comforting when nothing else will do,
Let a pie get you through Monday, which will be yum, not blue.

5

In a frame, I hold my successful feat,
A moment captured, oh so sweet.

Each glance brings back that gleaming pride,
A triumph that cannot be denied.

To see this picture brings such delight,
What would you choose to be forever in your sight?

If given a chance, which moment grand,
Would you frame with loving hand?

Would it be a passion that set your heart aflame?
Or a victory that brought you fame?

Perhaps a quiet, cherished embrace,
Or a journey to a distant place?

In this frame, we hold a piece of time,
A treasure trove, a chance to capture the sublime.

Choose your picture, hold it close to your heart,
A moment more precious than any piece of art.

6

Today, the window cleaner called to do his thing,
Positivity with him he did bring.

For clean windows, it's Feng Shui's delight,
Letting in clear energy, pure and bright.

Reflections crisp, inviting flow,
Harmony within, peace shall grow.

Just as windows gleam, so should we,
Clearing minds of clutter, setting thoughts free.

Negative emotions like dirt can cling,
Feel them, let them go, restore your zing.

Remove the grime, let positivity reign,
A fresh outlook on life, you shall gain.

7

The rhyming muse eludes me today,
Oh, please come back, I pray.

What can I do to be inspired?
Perhaps write about folks whom I've admired.

Maybe I'll use a famous quote,
A little hack, using words other people wrote.

What if I write about my favourite tune?
Or how I love the stars and moon?

I often extol the virtues of self-care,
Promoting kindness, I can't go wrong there.

There are plenty of ways in which to amuse,
It seems that after all this rhyming bug I can't lose. (*phew!*)

8

Come with me on a round-the-world tour,
There's no need to set foot outside your door.

From French kissing in Paris, we'll start our spree,
Then feast on a full English breakfast with glee.

In a Mexican stand-off, we'll play our part,
Before devouring Danish pastries, a sweet work of art.

Next, a game of Russian roulette, a risky affair,
But we'll laugh it off with daring flair.

Then it's off to Amsterdam, where we won't pay much,
For we're splitting bills, going Dutch, as such!

On our tour, we've been going full steam,
Time for bed, to contemplate the American Dream.

9

Brene Brown said, *Talk to yourself like you would talk to someone you love*,
Now, imagine you are being spoken to by an Angel from above.

It's time to be your own best mate,
With your internal dialogue, do not yourself berate.

Though at the idea of bigging yourself up you may balk,
Get into the habit of positive self-talk.

Though in the past, you may have heard a cruel voice,
The good news is now you have a choice.

Today, make a difference: choose a positive affirmation,
One to fill you with hope and elation.

With yourself, it's time to have an encouraging chat,
Then in time, my friend, you'll be feeling all that.

10

When life feels rough, like clay into a kiln we are thrown,
Fired and tested, feeling alone.

In the furnace of trials, we're shaped and spun,
Till a masterpiece emerges, once we're done.

Each challenge we face, a searing heat,
Moulding us strong, from our head to our feet.

Though the flames may scorch, and the ashes fly,
Within the inferno, our spirit can't die.

Through hardships endured, our character grows,
Like a sculpture unveiled, our beauty shows.

From the depths of struggle, we rise anew,
Transformed by the fire, bold and true.

So when life gets tough, embrace the flame's burn,
For within its heat, there's much to learn.

Like a phoenix, from the ashes we will rise,
A masterpiece crafted, resting now beneath cloudless skies.

11

Using Zoom for the first time was quite a shock for me,
For I'm such a confident person when I meet someone physically.

But, alas, with each pixel and each zoomed frame,
My insecurities rose: suddenly I was in the scrutinizing game.

I noticed my red cheeks, that prominent mole,
Suddenly I saw bits, not my lovely whole.

Cosmetic surgery, they say, is a booming trend.
Now, our every flaw we seek to mend.

We scrutinize every line and wrinkle we see,
Forgetting our essence and our true beauty.

Yet when we gaze at those we hold dear,
We don't see imperfections—their worth is clear.

We see laughter lines and eyes that shine bright,
We see love and warmth, pure and light.

So let's shift our focus, let's change our view,
And, with the eyes of an angel, look at ourselves anew.

Next time we have to face a Zoom call,
Let's smile, let's laugh, then we'll look the loveliest of all.

12

Jeffrey Deaver wrote, *It's a tough life and it's the little things that get us through the day.*
That made me think about the little things that help me on my way:

I like a morning coffee in my favourite mug,
Seeing a pal and getting an impromptu hug.

I appreciate things around me that are shiny and bright,
It's strange how a glittery pen can make my world feel right.

My umbrella isn't there just to protect me from the rain,
It's so pretty that, even when wet, it can make me smile again.

The note pad that I use to write down my shopping list,
Is so flowery and nice, it makes drudge fun, I'm sure you get the gist.

So if today, perhaps, you are struggling to smile,
Contemplate the things you love and let joy in, just for a little while.

13

I burn in the sun, a true English rose,
But of Helios' rays I am craving a dose.

Though I burn in his fiery gaze,
I yearn for spring's warm, golden phase.

Winter's chill, your frosty ways, bid adieu,
I've had enough, I want to see the back of you.

I dream of bare legs, oh so free,
Beneath the sky, by the sea,

As sunset hues paint elegantly,
I sip cocktails, contentedly.

So, Mr. Sunshine, with your golden glow,
Upon this English Rose bestow,

A touch of warmth, snowdrops please not snow,
Let spring's embrace begin to show.

For I'm done with winter's cold embrace,
I'm craving the sun upon my face.

Helios, please, give me a lingering look, not a glance,
Or I may be forced to do a little Sun Dance.

14

It's the season of giving up: Ramadan and Lent,
The spiritual intention is so very well meant.

There's plenty of things I could give up,
Such as ice-cold Prosecco, or creamy hot chocolate in a very large cup.

I think though I will try a different way,
Maybe give up on being hard on myself today.

Or stop saying *Yes* when I want to say *No*,
The seeds of assertiveness that would sow.

What about showing guilt the door?
Perhaps, for success in life, give up giving myself a score.

Good luck to all you making a spiritual sacrifice,
And cheers to me, with a glass of fizz, my favourite vice.

15

Roses are such lovely flowers,
Whether seen in the wild, or in garden bowers.

What an honour it would be to have one bear your name,
Unique like you, no two roses are the same.

Its oil rejuvenates your skin with a gentle kiss,
Its scent divine and feels like bliss.

Comforting, it gently caresses,
In its essence, all stress regresses.

A potion of solace, a touch of care,
In the embrace of roses rare.

So let us revel in their sweet embrace,
A flower that seems beyond time and space.

For in the loveliness of roses, we find,
Beauty, eternal, for heart and mind.

16

Today I'm leaving my little market town so pretty,
And heading off in to the big city.

To meet a pal who means the world to me,
Whose presence fills my heart with glee.

We've been friends for years and years,
And have seen each other through joy and tears.

We've navigated little bumps in the road,
And lightened each others, sometimes heavy, load.

She's a Burlesque dancer and each day I rhyme,
We connect though kindness time after time.

Our laughter has been ever present,
This friendship was truly Heaven-sent.

So watch out big city The Bubbly Girls are in town,
Fabulous, sparkly and of some renown!

17

In a land of the shamrock, St. Patrick did teach,
Bringing Christianity within Ireland's reach.

With a shamrock's leaves, the Trinity he'd show,
Three in one, faith's seeds to sow.

On St. Paddy's Day, we don green with glee,
Honorary Irish, as far as we can see.

For Ireland's the Emerald Isle, so fair,
And green keeps those leprechauns from our hair!

Raise a pint of Guinness, let's all cheer,
Ireland's famous drink, in our hearts held dear.

With laughter and merriment, we'll celebrate right,
With green on our backs, and a pint in sight!

So let's dance a jig and sing with delight,
On St. Patrick's Day, we'll party all night.

For the luck of the Irish we seek to embrace,
In this quirky, fun-filled, St. Paddy's Day space!

18

In the middle of the night, I heard an owl hooting.
It was a magical sound, there's no disputing.

For when the rest of the world was asleep,
Hearing nature so close was an experience so deep.

'Cause normally, man-made noise blocks out the sound,
Of the wonders of nature all around.

So, I forgive that little owl for the sleep it cost,
For a moment in the beauty of our world, I was lost.

19

When tasks pile high and stress feels vast,
Start small, my friend, don't rush too fast.

Pick one small thing and make it a delight,
With a pleasant start you will feel more bright.

Plan your dinner, or water a plant,
Small victories build; soon success will be evident.

With each little win, energy will brew,
Empowering you to tackle all that's due.

Reward yourself once tasks are done,
Have a treat and plan some fun.

Celebrate your victory over procrastination,
Let yourself feel that accomplishment elation.

For the war of the To-Do List you did win,
So now kick back, relax; that ain't no sin.

20

Today is the spring equinox, a day of balance,
Between light and dark, let's welcome this cosmic dance.

Take today to discover the balance within,
We need to be whole, in life, to win.

Embrace it all, the light and the dark.
We need both to generate the creative spark.

Meditate, reflect, and set intentions clear,
Confront the shadow—there's no need to fear.

With gratitude and joy, as we welcome the light,
On this Equinox, let us cherish both day and night.

By doing so, we will find our way,
To brighter tomorrows, come what may.

21

Today, for Aries folk, it's a Happy Birthday,
Bold and brash, they lead the way.

With fire in their eyes and spring in their stride,
Ariens have ambition they cannot hide.

Fiery and feisty, a force to behold,
Their passion and energy never grow old.

Quick to react, sometimes too fast,
Their impulsive nature creates an impression to last.

Adventure calls, they're always on the move,
Life's their playground, they've nothing to prove.

Independent souls, they blaze their own trail,
But patience? Well, that's a fairytale.

So here's to Aries, bold and bright,
Living life at full throttle, day and night.

Lady Gaga, one of the greatest stars there has ever been,
Shares this sign; Aries folk, never forgotten once seen.

22

In the midst of hustle I had to take a break,
Caught in the grip of a cold, my body did ache.

Today, I had to let the hours unfold,
Forced to step back, as the virus took hold.

But in this stillness, a truth emerged bright,
I'm more than the roles to which I hold on tight.

Not defined by my deeds, but the heart within,
A lesson learned as I let the day spin.

And amidst the sniffles, something grew,
I was able to craft a rhyme for you.

A testament clear, to the spirit within,
For when the body is weak the soul will always win.

Though tasks may wait and deadlines loom,
I'll cherish this pause, dispelling the gloom.

For in taking the time, I find what is true,
I'm not just what I do, but who I am, too.

23

When you venture on a walk,
There's always one thing of which you'll talk:

The weather. Not just a condition in the atmosphere,
But a thing to discuss to bring folks near.

Rain at Christmas; at Easter snow,
It seems of our celebrations Nature is not in the know.

She won't play ball with our grand design,
Still, who are we to argue with the divine?

When we face together the storms that rage,
It's a chance for us with others to engage.

So, let's embrace the weather, whatever it may be,
For it brings us closer, you and me.

Through rain or shine, we can have a chat,
Bonding over the weather, in July wearing a woolly hat!

24

On National Cocktail Day, let's line up the bar,
With libations which show us who we are.

Some prefer Sex on the Beach, fruity and bold,
With lips to kiss and hands to hold.

Old Fashioned folks, they're classic and refined,
Sipping with grace, with style they're aligned.

Manhattan sophisticates, with a touch of class,
Their taste for the finer things is unsurpassed.

Piña colada lovers, laid-back and carefree,
Their mantra is simple: *Life's a beach, you see!*

Espresso Martini fans, fuelled by caffeine,
With energy boundless, at the centre of any scene.

So on this festive day, let's toast with cheer,
To cocktails that define us, year after year.

Whether shaken or stirred, in a glass or a cup,
Cheers to National Cocktail Day! Bottoms up!

25

Beneath the glow of the full *Worm Moon* light,
We embrace the cycle of renewal tonight.

For just as the worm heals itself in the embrace of the earth,
Our wounded selves can experience rebirth.

This moon is also known as the *Moon of Sap*,
As our energy rises, we can escape winter's trap.

Coinciding with Holi's colourful display,
Where joy and laughter lead the way.

In the streets, with family and strangers too,
A celebration that allows us to renew.

Under the light of the moon, let's sing and dance,
And rejoice in the gift of the *Worm Moon*: a second chance.

26

The apple is a fruit so versatile,
With myriad ways to make you smile.

It can be used in chutneys, puddings, or a pie,
Producing cider to put a glint in your eye.

You can munch on a *Jazz*, or *Cox's Orange Pippin*,
On a warm summer's day it's juice you'll be sippin'.

Apple Cider vinegar is now on trend,
To all manner of ills a cure it does lend.

Whether a *Granny Smith*, a *Laxton's Fortune*, or *Pink Lady*,
Let's cherish this gift of nature from a magic tree.

27

In fields of gold, where daffodils sway,
Marie Curie's cause lights up the way.

With hearts of courage, they tirelessly strive,
To bring solace and comfort, to keep hope alive.

Through the Great Daffodil Appeal, a beacon gleams,
For those in darkness, it's more than it seems.

Yellow petals, a symbol of light,
In their darkest hour, shining bright.

For those with illness, in their final fight,
Marie Curie's love is a guiding light.

Their care and support, like daffodils bloom,
Bringing warmth and nurture, dispersing gloom.

With every purchase, a gesture so small,
Supporting those in need, love for all.

So let's rally together, in this noble cause,
With daffodils in hand, let's give applause.

For Marie Curie's appeal, let's unite,
Bringing courage, in the darkest night.

28
I wonder what your hair says about you,
Is it short, long; red or blue?

Mine is short, funky and violet,
That says a lot about me, I bet.

Some may think it's daring and bold;
I think it's a sight to behold.

And though it does make quite a statement,
Having it this way I have an over-riding intent.

Which is to avoid faff in the morning with the hair dryer,
Though if I said I didn't enjoy looking unique, I'd be a liar.

I think I will keep this style until I'm very old,
Even though it's useless at keeping out the cold.

For, once cut, a little gel is all is all it does require,
To become a work of art that some admire.

29
Today is not just any Friday, it is Good Friday.
But why *Good* if it commemorates how a man died in such a terrible way?

Well it's not a as simple as that you see,
For whatever our religion, this day has a message for you and me.

Which is: within suffering is contained great hope,
A thought that with our own trials can help us cope.

Our ordeals need not be in vain,
Those words have such a sweet refrain.

For whatever you are enduring, or pain you're in,
It will never ever touch your spirit within.

For like Jesus, you are not just your body but so much more,
So, on this holy day, let's rise and show despair the door.

30
Today, when out and about, I went to spend a penny,
In the queue for the loo, I met a girl called Jenny.

Who looked so fab, I just had to declare,
You look amazing, your clothes and hair!

Do you know, friend, it made her day,
And made see herself in a positive way.

She said, *I don't think of myself as looking nice.*
Girlfriend, I said, *You better think twice!*

After telling her that she looked all that,
We had a lovely uplifting chat.

So remember to be brave and give someone a compliment,
For to them, it could be the gift they need, Heaven-sent.

31
It's Easter and time to greet,
The Bunny who hops with nimble feet,

And brings us Easter eggs of every hue,
Delivering joy to me and you.

We each have our favourite Easter egg treat,
The one that just can't be beat.

Grown-ups become kids, full of glee,
Hunting for eggs 'neath every tree.

Enjoying their discovered chocolate treasures,
Restraint is forgotten for one of life's great pleasures.

So let's rejoice and have some fun,
Happy Easter to everyone!

April

1

Today there's so much pressure to look stylish and cool,
Well, for one day, let's become an April Fool.

For, dear friend, it's true what they say:
Fun and play is the angel's way.

And that when we approach life with a lighter touch,
We can let go of the things that bother us much.

So, today, find something to make your heart feel light,
Do something silly to make your world seem bright.

Turn up for work in fancy dress,
And abandon the need to impress.

Instead of walking, skip into town,
You'll raise a smile, only a few will frown.

Laughter you see is the greatest medicine,
So be an April Fool today, it's really quite Zen.

P.S. Write a rhyme that makes no sense,
Everyone loves a bit of nonsense!

2

The animal kingdom, so diverse,
Lends itself to phrases in many a verse.

A fly on the wall eavesdrops with glee,
While monkeying around can be very naughty.

Hungry as a horse, with a ravenous bite,
No room to swing a cat, in this chaotic sight.

There's the snake in the grass, oh so sly,
And the elephant in the room, hard to deny.

Fit as a butcher's dog, ready for a run,
A sly old fox, always fun.

Maybe you're as wise as an owl,
Or a little chicken, like the timid farmyard fowl.

Whatever you are, as proud as a Peacock you should be,
So a little bird told me!

3

In hues of wonder, the rainbow gleams,
More than just colours; more than it seems.

A symbol of promise after the Flood's great plight,
A covenant from God, shining so bright.

It's diversity's flag, a tapestry vast,
In each vibrant hue, a story is cast.

In *The Wizard of Oz*, it arcs over the sky,
A pathway to dreams, where bluebirds fly.

Somewhere over the rainbow, dreams come true,
A quest for happiness, for me and for you.

I remember the day, as I walked down the aisle,
To the tune of that song, it made me smile.

Through moments of loss, when darkness seemed near,
A rainbow appeared, wiping away every tear.

Let it remind us, when trials we face,
Of the miraculous promise of love and grace.

In every rainbow a story of hope,
A journey to joy and a way to cope.

A magic jewel in this world of strife,
The rainbow is a gift, a sign, and a wonder to enhance our life.

4

What is your favourite sound, the one you love to hear?
Mine's my husband's key in the door, telling me he's near.

I also love bird song on a springtime morn,
Or a friend's text when I'm feeling so forlorn.

There are so many sounds that give my heart a lift,
So I cherish my hearing as a lovely gift.

Take note today of what you hear and maybe stop a while,
Notice the sounds that you love and that make you smile.

The purr of a cat, the ocean waves, never fail to console,
Cherish the sounds around you—nourishment for your soul.

5

I love the saying, *Don't exercise; accessorize*,
For a new handbag always puts a sparkle in my eyes.

When I say new, it doesn't have to be one that's all the rage,
I'm a big fan of a charity shop find and love vintage.

A *Lulu Guinness* would look great on my arm,
But a lovely bargain bag would hold equal charm.

For whether *Primark*, *Burberry*, *Prada*, or *Chanel*,
Sometimes it's really hard to tell.

The thing about a bag is no sizing is required,
To make a statement and be admired.

Tote, hobo, or clutch, I love them all,
With a new bag on my arm, watch me swagger and stand tall.

6

I hate wind—not the farting or burping kind.
It's windy weather that messes with my mind.

I can see the point of a shower of rain,
But to me, wind is just a pain.

I suppose a cooling breeze is okay,
Wind mostly, though, just disrupts the day.

I don't need wind to blow my cobwebs away,
When the wind blows, at home I'll stay.

I don't even want the winds of change to blow,
No thanks—I'll choose which way I go.

I have no urge to fly a kite,
Yes, me and the wind just don't sit right.

7

In a land of glitz and sparkly lights,
Fifty years ago, in Eurovision's sights,

A Swedish band with a tune so bright,
Wowed the crowd and stole the night.

Claiming victory for all to see,
They went on to fill our hearts with glee.

With tunes such as *Mama Mia* and *Dancing Queen*,
A more captivating group there's never been.

Now half a century has passed us by,
But Abba's magic still lights up the sky.

So let's raise a toast, let's all enthuse,
Thank You for the Music, Abba, always an antidote for the blues.

8

In our lives, we've all had a sliding door moment,
When we had to choose, then not relent.

One step to the left: a journey anew,
Or veer to the right: a different avenue.

Mine was whether or not to go out one night,
I did and met the man who made my future bright.

Another time, I turned down a property,
Then felt it was the one for me.

It's easy to regret our choice,
So much harder to rejoice.

A job we didn't take; a love we let pass by.
Pondered upon, we yearn and sigh.

Let's trust, though, that our path was Heaven-sent,
Cherish where we are now, a gift, the present.

Pantone's colour of the year, *Peach Fuzz*, a fruity delight,
Soft, warm, and soothing: peach is a gentle light.

Using the power of colour therapy, its magic we can deploy,
To bring calmness and joy to our world with ease and joy.

Peach whispers of sweetness, of tender embrace,
It fills every space with a comforting grace.

Adorn your walls with its soft, soothing glow,
Creating sanctuaries where tranquillity may flow.

Wear a little peach and you'll look great,
With others, you'll connect and communicate.

Peach symbolizes compassion, empathy, and care,
In a world full of chaos, it's a breath of fresh air.

So let's welcome this colour, both subtle and bold,
Be it in decor, or attire, let its healing unfold.

With peach all around, let worries unwind,
For in its gentle presence, true solace we find.

10

It's National Farm Animals Day, so let's remember with glee,
The joy of singing Old McDonald's farm, while sitting on someone's knee.

When we were little, we loved the sounds animals made,
Moo, *Baaa*, and *Cluck*, enjoying the milk and the chucky eggs they laid.

But as we grow, our appreciation must expand,
To care for these beings, let's stretch out our hand.

Eggs, milk, and meat, they sustain us every day,
Yet some animals suffer in conditions far from okay.

Though we enjoy the bounty they provide,
It's essential that their welfare is never denied.

We mustn't turn a blind eye to their plight,
For their well-being, we must continue to fight.

On this special day, let's take a stand,
By signing a petition or giving a helping hand.

To charities that strive for better conditions, let's donate,
Ensuring farm animals have a brighter fate.

On National Farm Animals Day, in our hearts let's hold these creatures near,
Let's pledge to protect them, year after year.

11

In life, we often find ourselves climbing hills,
Metaphorical peaks, testing our wills.

Sometimes it's illness, loss, or financial strain,
Obstacles looming and causing us pain.

But with every challenge there's a way,
To ascend those slopes, come what may.

Friends are the ropes that help us ascend,
Their support is a lifeline on which we depend.

Step by step, we make our ascent,
We conquer each stage with strength and courage Heaven-sent.

Resting a while to catch our breath,
Gathering strength to face the test.

Through the struggle, we start again,
With the future in sight, hope is our refrain.

Looking back, we see how far we've come,
The battles fought and the victories won.

Our minds, bodies, and spirits, stronger than before,
For overcoming the challenges that knocked at our door.

So let us remember, when faced with the hill,
That with friendship's help and perseverance, we will,

Rise above the hardships, emerge triumphant and free,
Ready to face whatever life's hills may be.

12

Friday, oh Friday, the day we adore,
When we show our workday worries the door.

Derived from Freya, the Norse for Venus, the love goddess,
A day that we long for, venerate, and bless.

But who can we show some love to on this day?
To brighten their path in every way?

To our colleague, who's pushing through strife,
A smile or kind word can change their life.

To our spouse, weary from the week's slog,
Offer a kiss, perchance an unexpected snog.

To our friend, feeling lonely and blue,
A call or a visit could uplift them too.

Yet amidst spreading love to others, don't forget.
To remember yourself, to nurture, not neglect.

For a weekend of joy and rest you deserve,
To replenish your spirit and regain your verve.

So let's embrace Friday with love so true,
And spread it around to me and to you.

For in giving and receiving, we find,
The happiness that leaves all worries behind.

13

In the silent hush of the night's embrace,
I lay in bed seeking elusive grace.

But sleep, a trickster, eludes my grasp,
Leaving me tangled in its restless clasp.

The clock ticks on, with its relentless chime,
As I count the hours, lost in time.

Thoughts whirl and dance: a ceaseless parade;
In the caverns of my mind they cascade.

I've tried the remedies—every one:
Lavender's scent when the day is done,

Tech detoxes and hot showers too,
Still, sleep remains a distant view.

With each passing hour, mounting frustration,
As I try to solve the problems of the nation.

And as dawn breaks, I rise once more,
Shattered, but ready to explore.

The day ahead, with its promise bright,
Hoping for better rest tonight.

But alas, the cycle repeats,
As I lay in bed, counting my heart's beats.

For sleep remains a stranger to me,
What else could I try? Perhaps a little herbal tea.

14

Today we are warned of the dangers of everything.
Oh dear, the things we are told are bad make my heart sing.

When we eat, we are told care we should take,
But I have to confess that I love a cupcake.

Before you pour that glass of wine, you should think,
Alas, I love a glass of Prosecco to drink.

And as for gambling, that's a real no-no,
That means my lottery ticket has to go.

We're even told what fairy tales and films might trigger us.
But I really don't understand the fuss.

So what's a good-time girl like me to do?
Listen to the warnings and make her golden life blue?

No, I think as I am, I will carry on,
'Cause my life ain't safe, but it's certainly fun.

15

Life's a fairground, a whirl of delight,
With twists and turns, we hold on tight.

On the Big Dipper, we rise and fall,
Feeling the rush and embracing it all.

Haunted by demons from our yesteryears,
We ride the Ghost Train, facing our fears.

Through darkened tunnels, we journey inside,
Confronting the shadows, angels we pray are by our side.

Stress spins us round on the Waltzer's track,
Dizzy and wild, we'd like to backtrack.

Sometimes we find a moment to rest,
Hooking a Duck, we are at our best.

Like a sharpshooter on the Rifle Range,
We aim for our dreams and feel our luck change.

With steady hands, we hit the bullseye,
Winning a prize, with joy we cry.

Yet in the midst of this carnival of life,
Amidst all the joy and occasional strife,

We find that the secret to peace is to know,
To enjoy the ride, we must go with the flow.

16

In winter's grip Clematis sleeps, a dormant sight,
Cut to its roots, seeming to lose it's fight.

But in spring, a miracle is found:
Emerging strong, the Clematis shoots break ground.

Just like the vine, we too suffer harsh cuts,
But from our roots, new strength erupts.

In life's pruning, we find resilience true,
From setbacks, we rise, blooming anew.

17

Broccoli and beetroot are both hailed as superfoods,
But which Magic Food is guaranteed to lift your mood?

The food to which you always turn,
When for some comfort you do yearn.

My hubby's is fried egg on toast,
That's the thing he craves the most.

When he's ill or his day is blue,
Only egg on toast will do.

Mine is nachos or a cream bun,
They're sure to restore my sense of fun.

So whilst it's true some foods our ills might cure,
Let's salute those that nurture our souls, the ones we adore.

For though Superfoods may contain many a vitamin and antioxidant,
Our Magic Foods provide nurture that is Heaven-sent.

18

In poetry's realm, a vibrant sea,
Diverse forms dance, wild and free.

From sonnets structured, tightly bound,
To haikus brief, with nature's sound.

Odes sing praises, passions ignite,
Epics stretch far, tales take flight.

Acoustic pastoral, whispers of peace,
Each form a world, a masterpiece.

Yet amidst this tapestry, diverse and sublime,
I find my solace in simple rhyme.

For in its cadence, a magic spell,
Where deep truths dwell, so clear, so well.

With rhythm's pulse, like a beating heart,
It paints emotions, a subtle art.

In its simplicity, depths unfurl,
A melody of thought, a lyrical swirl.

So while preferences vary, styles abound,
In the realm of rhyme, my love is found.

For within its lines, profound and plain,
Lies a beauty timeless, a gentle refrain.

19

In the hustle of life, where battles abound,
There's always a warrior to be found.

In daily life, they are not always recognised,
For it is often fame and money that are idolized.

In daily endeavours, unseen warriors quietly strive,
With steadfast resolve, they keep dreams alive.

A job they despise, yet they labour each day,
To provide for their kin, the course they will stay.

Through illness and pain, warriors bravely endure,
Their spirit unwavering, though their body is sore.

In the crowd, there's one, overcoming fright,
Shyness conquered, they step into the light.

And those who reveal their true selves at last,
Breaking free of judgments from the past.

Their authenticity, a beacon so bright,
Illuminating paths, once hidden from sight.

Now, take a moment, look deep inside,
And ask where you've fought, and where you've cried.

For in the battles we face, big and small,
There lies the heart of a warrior in us all.

20

Today, my friends, our hearts are full,
With birthday wishes for those born under the sign of the bull.

With traits so solid and virtues bright,
Their full lips and expressive eyes are quite a sight.

Hard-headed they may be, it's true,
But their resolve and strength see them through.

Down-to-earth, grounded in their way,
Guiding others through night and day.

Tenacious souls, they never yield,
Their steadfast spirit an unbreakable shield.

Sensual beings with senses keen,
In restaurants, indulging they are often seen.

So here's to those born under this sign,
With a will as sturdy as an ancient vine.

They share their path with Adele's sweet song,
And The Rock's might, steadfast and strong.

Happy Birthday, dear Taurus, may your year be grand,
With joys aplenty and blessings at hand.

21

Extroverts and Introverts, though as different as can be,
Both have lovely qualities, if you look you'll see.

One finds strength in solitude, calm and serene;
The other in social circles, where they're often seen.

Introverts recharge with solitary peace,
In nature's embrace or a cosy fleece.

Extroverts are the life of the party, you know,
They're the ones dancing on tables, putting on a show.

Introverts watch quietly, sipping on their beer,
Always ready and willing to lend a listening ear.

Extroverts thrive on social scenes, it's true,
Their strength lies in connections, old and new.

Introverts delve deep within,
Thinking before their words begin.

You'll spot an extrovert with a laugh that's loud,
All about the *Va-Va-Voom* and standing out from the crowd.

But introverts, they're more the observing kind,
Taking in the world with a thoughtful mind.

Extrovert or introvert, your qualities matter,
For there's a time for quiet and a time for chatter.

We need all kinds of folk in this world, you see,
That's the thought of the day from little old extrovert me!

22

In the ocean of life, we sail each day,
Navigating the waters, each in our own way.

We're all in the same boat, that's for sure,
Trying not to rock it, but wanting more.

When the waves are rough and the currents churn,
Stay steady, my friend, and you will learn.

With a bit of luck and wind in your sail,
You'll reach calmer seas and will prevail.

Though the tide will rise and fall,
With perseverance, you'll overcome it all.

Batten down the hatches, weather the storm,
For brighter skies await in the morn.

Seek friends who will help to tide you over,
Soon you'll find you'll be in clover.

Then set your sheets to the wind and celebrate,
Life's great voyage and being your own first mate.

23

In days of yore, in a land of old,
St. George rode forth, valiant and bold.

A dragon fierce, with fiery breath,
Threatened the kingdom with fear and death.

With lance in hand, armour shining head to toe,
He faced the beast, a most terrifying foe.

Neither fear nor doubt could diminish his soul,
For to serve and liberate was his noble goal.

The dragon roared with rage and ire,
But St. George pressed on, his spirit afire.

With a mighty blow, he struck the beast.
Killing it, heralding in a celebration feast.

In our lives, we face our dragons too,
Fear, doubt, and anxiety can pursue.

We wield our own sword of courage and hope,
Vanquishing our demons; victory within our scope.

Let us march forth with confidence high,
Then our monsters we can defy.

For though to sainthood we may not aspire,
We can slay our doubt and achieve our heart's desire.

24

Coffee is my favourite drink,
Apparently, it helps you think.

I drink decaf, so I'm not sure that's the case,
Still, I love my coffee, I think it's ace.

It gets my day off to a civilized start,
Bringing order even when chaos reigns within my heart.

In the afternoon, it gives me a little break,
Often accompanied by a naughty cake.

Of course, it has to be made in a cafetière,
It's my way of showing myself some care.

It has to be ground, no instant will do,
Thank you, coffee, my ritual, my treat, my special brew.

25

I live in a town with an elderly population,
I admit their slower pace sometimes causes irritation.

When I'm in haste, with somewhere to be,
Their shuffle can feel like a hindrance to me.

In this scenario are lessons to be had,
For it's patience and kindness that make the heart glad.

So though their pace may try my will,
In their journey, I find still…

A reminder to relax and be,
Not rush, but take time to truly see.

They're not mere obstacles, but lives well-lived,
With wisdom, love, and stories to give.

So, I'll take a breath, and slow my stride,
Cherishing moments, walking by their side.

For in this town, which elders grace,
There's beauty found in each patient pace.

26

In vast skies, day and night,
Dance clouds of myriad hues and light.

Some drift like cotton, soft and bright,
While others loom with a storm's fierce might.

Oh, how I love the fluffy white,
Pillows in heavens, such a sight!

But when the grey clouds blanket the day,
They dim the sun and take my joy away.

On a scorching day, clouds can be our shelter,
From the sun's rays, underneath which we swelter.

These are the days when the sun is a bane,
And we wish for the clouds to bring us rain.

So, let us marvel at the sky,
Where clouds in all their splendour lie.

Whether cirrus or nimbus, they have their place,
Look carefully and in them you may behold an angel's face.

27

I have an appointment today, and it might be tough.
So this little rhyme will have to be enough.

Though short, it still contains a message true,
Which is that there are times you need to prioritise you.

Times to let others take the strain,
To open up about your pain.

Instead of giving until you empty your tank,
For deposits, open up your own love bank.

Just hang on, you need to find a way,
Have hope for tomorrow, which truly is another day.

28

In a world full of bubbles, my heart finds its glee,
Sparkling wine's cork popping—a toast to revelry.

Clinking glasses with a friend,
Celebrations that never end.

In the bath's embrace, a soothing sight,
With bubbles swirling, pure delight.

A sanctuary, serene and calm,
In fragrant foam, I find my balm.

When feeling down, bubbles I will blow,
A childhood charm, a magic show.

They float and twirl, without a care,
A rainbow's gleam, they gladly share.

In sparkling wine, baths, or the playful kind,
Bubbles bring joy, delight and succour to my mind.

So if today your life seems a little flat,
Embrace the bubbles, for they are therapy, that's a fact.

29

In a world where dreams take flight,
I yearn for luxury—a lavish delight.

A train journey grand, a feast for my soul,
Moments of opulence, a cherished goal.

But as I dream of travelling in style,
I should take time to think a while.

For some, it's basic needs that are,
Regarded as luxury, for they have to walk far,

To get water, to them a treasure rare,
A luxury beyond compare.

Whilst I plan lavish menus in my head,
Some struggle to get their daily bread.

So as I dream, let me be aware of others' pain,
And aim for a true and lasting gain.

For nice things are great, but the truest pleasure
Is kindness in our hearts—a luxurious treasure.

30

In lands afar, different traditions thrive,
That can help us in life we strive.

From Japan's forests, so lush and green,
Comes *Shinrin-Yoku*, a tranquil scene.

Bathing in nature, amidst the trees,
Brings peace and calm, with every breeze.

Then over to Denmark, where cosiness reigns,
Hygge they call it, where comfort sustains.

With blankets so soft and candles aglow,
Finding contentment, enveloped in a fluffy throw.

Ice baths in Scandi countries are a thing,
They don't appeal though, or make my heart sing.

In cold water, I don't want to freeze,
So I'll stick to *Hygge* after I've done *Shinrin-Yoku* and talked to the trees!

May

1

Today May Day arrives with its vibrant cheer,
With promise of a blossoming year.

Join hands and hearts, around the maypole we'll sway,
And in colourful ribbons weave and play.

Seek out the merry Morris dancers in their array,
Their bells and steps, a joyous display.

As dawn breaks, greet the rising sun,
Celebrating spring and its days of fun.

Craft a crown of blooms, in a whimsical way,
Adorn yourself, be queen for the day!

So here's to May Day and its sights so bright,
Let May Day encourage and delight!

2

On waking today, everything felt wrong.
I didn't know who I was; where did I belong?

With things to do, how was I going to get by?
Well, I sat down and had myself a little cry.

For I'm a firm believer in the power of tears,
To help ease your pain and wash away your fears.

Tears mean that you are taking care of you:
They help cleanse you and face the world anew.

After my cry, on the day, I was ready to take a chance.
I got up, put the radio on, and had a little dance.

So don't be scared if one day you feel sad and blue.
Have a cry; tears will heal you, I promise you, it's true.

3

Today, I marked my X, a solemn task,
Five minutes out of my day—not a lot to ask.

To remember struggles past, a legacy dear,
Of those who fought, year after year.

Their cries for justice in that valiant fight,
Echo in every ballot and every right.

So as I placed my X, I made a vow,
To honour the past and to shape the now.

For not to vote is an act absurd,
When so many sacrificed so that my voice would be heard.

For voting isn't just a choice we make,
But a way to shape our future at stake.

To create a world where all voices count:
When using democracy, problems we surmount.

So let us cherish this sacred right,
With every ballot, with all our might.

For in our hands, is Destiny's key,
In the act of voting, we are e truly free.

4

On May the Fourth, let's shout with glee,
May the Force be With You, and also with me!

It's Star Wars Day, a cosmic delight,
That helps us tell wrong from right.

As we celebrate this quirky date in May.
Let's ponder which character we could play:

Would you be Yoda, little, cute and green,
Or Han Solo, daring and keen?

Princess Leia, brave and sassy?
Or Luke Skywalker, young, cool and classy.

Whoever you choose, embrace Star Wars day,
The force is with you, let your inner hero out to play.

5

Through trials dire, they're a guiding light,
In their embrace, let imagination take flight.

The Lion, the Witch and the Wardrobe, is beyond compare,
A tale of courage and hope in despair.

When little, I escaped to Narnia's land,
Dreaming of holding Mr. Tumnus' hand.

Tales of the City is a peerless treat,
Full of heart with an urban beat.

Through laughter, tears, and city lights,
Whispering, *You're not alone in these nights.*

M. Scott Peck's *The Road Less Travelled*, I found,
Is a book that offers insights profound.

It showed the way and presented a view,
Transforming my thoughts to see the world anew.

Books can soothe a troubled soul,
And help you heal and become whole.

For in their realm of ink and page,
Books enthral, guiding every stage.

6

If someone said you were beige, it may be an insult to you,
But here's a different point of view:

For in our world, beige has its place,
In fact, at times, it can be quite ace.

In the world of colour, beige provides a backdrop,
Enabling other colours to shine and pop.

In life, too, if we were all vibrant in our display,
It could prove stressful day after day.

For, sometimes, we need an oasis of calm;
Beige people can provide a comforting balm.

Search deep and I'm sure you would agree,
We need all kinds of folks for life's rich tapestry.

Let's honour the folk we describe as beige;
In fact, for once, let's make beige all the rage!

7

I love to shop till I drop,
A favourite haunt is a charity shop.

I get such a lot of pleasure,
Hunting down a bargain treasure.

I like turning my back on corporate greed,
Helping those who are in need,

Keeping the less fortunate in mind,
Doing my bit to be kind.

When encountering a volunteer,
I want to give them a great big cheer,

For giving their time to help out,
Though in giving they are blessed, no doubt.

Visit a charity shop, it's a great thing to do.
Now excuse me, I've another rail to rummage through!

8

I used to love to ride a donkey by the seashore,
Though, I've since learned that to the donkey there is so much more,

Than providing seaside fun,
It seems throughout the world their work is never done.

With ears like sails, and a bray so grand,
They're the unsung heroes of the land.

In fields of green, or on paths that wind and knot,
They carry loads and endure such a lot.

From mountains high, to valleys low,
Donkeys trek where few dare go.

Though useful and loyal in so many ways,
They are sometimes abandoned at the end of their days.

So, next time you see a donkey in sight,
Pause for a moment, consider their plight.

Let's not overlook this humble friend,
Whose value knows no end.

From rides at the beach to burdens borne,
Donkeys, carried in our hearts, not left forlorn.

9

As I look out of my window, I can see a gorgeous plant.
I call it gorgeous now, but it used to make me rant.

It was big, bushy and full.
It didn't flower and was very dull.

Suddenly, though, it has put on a show,
Of purple blooms that almost glow.

So it has to be conceded,
That a little patience is what was needed.

In our lives too, it might take time,
For us to bloom, so here's the message of my rhyme:

Don't give up on yourself, keep believing in that dream,
For things are not always as they seem.

One day you will burst into flower,
Having endured an April shower.

To others, you will bring delight,
Because, like my plant, you shine bright.

10

You want to write and get it right,
But the fear of judgement invokes such fright.

The key is to treat the task as fun,
Then you're own approval you'll have won.

There's really no one looking over your shoulder,
Remembering this will make you bolder.

So pick up that pen, tap on that key,
And shout, *The only person I wanna please is ME, ME, ME!!!*

11

Gather 'round, folks, for a Eurovision delight,
Where nations collide, making spirits bright.

When we ask that *Love Shine a Light*, it's a sight to see,
As stars twinkle and shimmer, it's a great party.

We remember *Making Your Mind Up* and *Puppet on a String*,
Praying that this night a result will bring.

Though *Space Man* didn't deliver,
Round the world it sent a shiver.

As Sam showed that it's not about winning,
Through opening his heart, he left the world grinning.

So many years ago Lulu sang,
Giving us a win with *Boom Bang-a-Bang*.

In the '70s our hearts were filled with glee,
By a joyful tune: *Save Your Kisses for Me*.

Eurovision, such a friendly fight,
Helps us forget our troubles for just one night.

So let's support Olly as he sings in tune and loud,
Come on Olly do us proud!

12

This week, a friend visited from afar.
She's a warrior and a superstar,

Someone who, though not a celebrity,
Is an inspiration and means the world to me.

She's had her share of trouble and strife,
Winning her very own *Race for Life*.

To sit and chat, we found a nice churchyard,
Talking of life and how it's sometimes hard.

Though the church was closed, our minds were not;
We connected and explored such a lot.

We laughed and had such fun,
Recounting battles fought and won.

I realised that the Divine is not found in any building or place,
But in our hearts, a sacred space.

13

If you were to pick one crystal, what would it be?
Is a question often asked of me.

I never, ever, hesitate,
For Rose Quartz can be everybody's best mate.

It helps to mend a broken heart,
And can give your self-esteem a kick start.

With ongoing stress, it will help you deal;
When holding it, comfort and calm is what you'll feel.

It can help with looking for love;
From self-doubt, you will rise above.

Forget being left on the proverbial shelf;
Rose Quartz's greatest gift is to help you love yourself.

14
If I dwelt on all the frogs I kissed,
And the times to say, *Get lost*, I missed,

I could feel quite low, make myself sad,
But I've got a 6ft blue-eyed reason to be glad.

All the times I whined and pined,
Led me to a prince, who wined and dined.

One day I woke up and smelled the coffee,
If I wanted love I had to start with me.

For if you want another to fall for you,
You've gotta cheer yourself on in all you do.

Acknowledge your importance, and your worth,
Claim your unique spot on the Earth.

To hurt and pain learn to say No,
Then one day, in the arms of love, you will bask and glow.

15
In a world of treats, oh so sweet,
There's one for me that can't be beat:

Chocolate, oh what joy it does bring,
A symphony of silk, it makes my heart sing!

From dreamy milk, to dark so deep,
At any hour, from dawn to sleep,

In cocoa's embrace I find my bliss,
Chocolate, my friend, you never miss!

When life's troubles start to cling,
I reach for chocolate, that magical thing.

So here's to Chocolate, my sweet delight,
Thanks for making my world tasty and bright!

16

In life's relentless dance, resilience is key,
Preparing for challenges, for what's yet to be.

In the quiet moments, in the routines we sow,
We gather strength for when the storms blow.

Exercise, meditation, friends at our side,
These pillars of resilience help us abide.

In the face of trials, we'll stand tall and strong,
Fortitude our armour, against all that's wrong.

For in life's journey, challenges will appear,
But, with preparation, we'll have nothing to fear.

Our routines stand firm, like anchors, true,
Guiding us back to the path we once knew.

So let's embrace these practices, come what may,
For the strength they provide in every way.

When problems loom and skies turn grey,
Resilience whispers: We'll find a way.

17

One's body is not just a shell,
It's the source of expressions we use as well.

When we chat, we might see eye-to-eye,
In love you get itchy feet and say *Bye-bye*.

If you're ignored, given the cold shoulder,
You can choose to shrink, or fight back bolder.

You might need a friend who's all ears for your woes,
And will offer advice on your highs and lows.

Though some may look down their nose with a sigh,
Remember, there's room for all under this sky.

With a finger in every pie, all the options we explore,
Sometimes biting our tongue when we'd like to say more.

I hope you've enjoyed this rhyme and think it is grand,
Because, at rhyming, I'm an old hand.

18

The nursery rhyme, O! What a delight,
With characters so vivid and bright.

Humpty Dumpty was daring to sit on that wall,
But, sadly, took a tumble and had a great fall.

With hope in their hearts, Jack and Jill went up that hill,
But, alas! Jack banged his head and they both took a spill.

To make matters worse, their water mission was a fail,
For not a drop ended up in their pail.

Mary had a little lamb, so sweet,
Everywhere she went, you could hear it bleat.

It followed her merrily, without a frown,
Around the village, or into town.

Hickory Dickory Dock, the mouse so fit,
Ran up the clock but when it struck one, that was it.

Incy Wincy Spider, climbed up the spout,
Down came the rain, washing her out.

But Incy Wincy didn't mope,
She climbed up again, with a new hope.

With laughter, lessons, and joy to share,
Nursery rhymes, forever fair!

19

I'm currently looking for a new nest,
Would new build, or character, be best?

Do I go for a state-of-the-art?
Or an oldie that would tug at my heart?

A turnkey property might be nice;
Though a fixer-upper may suffice.

Does it matter if the *décor* is not to my taste?
I don't want to repent at leisure, and choose with haste.

Hmm, I think I need a new way of looking at this,
For my home is really where I find my bliss.

And bliss can be found wherever I roam,
For it's in my soul that I make my home.

As long as I keep that in mind,
Then my nest, within, I'll always find.

20

On Be a Millionaire Day, let's reflect and see,
The treasures in life that come naturally.

Health is our wealth, a gift so grand,
With strength and vitality at our command.

Love is a jewel that shines so bright,
A heart full of warmth; a beacon of light.

Friendship's a bond, unbreakable and true,
Through thick and thin, it sees us through.

A home is a haven, a comforting nest,
Where memories are made and we find our rest.

These blessings abound, they're all around;
In the simple joys, true riches are found.

Yes, money's useful, it's clear to see,
It buys some comfort and luxury;

But our greatest treasures, as we are taught,
Are those which cannot be bought.

21

Happy birthday, dear Gemini, at this sunny time of year,
A time to celebrate the twins, who bring us so much cheer.

With flexible minds and extrovert ways,
You light up our lives in countless, clever, displays.

Quick-witted and curious, you talk to anyone,
From happy hours to dinner parties, you bring the fun.

Dancing through life with passions that abound,
With friends a plenty, like a butterfly, you flit around.

Though indecisive at times, your curiosity's grand,
You juggle so much with a confident hand.

Playful and smart, you're a joy to behold,
Your always there with a tale to be told.

You share this day with legends, both Mel B and Mr. T,
A sign of greatness in your stars, for all the world to see.

22

I thought I'd be helpful today and write you a list,
Of things not to do when you're p**sed:

Don't go on the Internet to have a browse,
You'll end up buying that expensive blouse.

Don't put a picture of yourself on Facebook,
Staggering about just ain't a good look.

Don't send a text to your ex,
It may end in a regretful night of sex.

Don't call your boss to tell them what you think,
They want a pro, not someone who succumbs to drink.

Don't decide to argue with your mate,
Words said now are bound to grate.

Finally, though you think you are a poet with the most,
Don't think that others will appreciate your drunken post.

23

Today's full moon, known as the *Blossom Moon* by some,
Heralds days of joy to come.

A turning point in nature's dance;
A magic time to take your chance.

Let this moon's energy ignite,
Your hidden dreams and thoughts tonight.

Dig out clothes, bold and bright,
Let creativity take its flight.

Tend your garden, plant your seeds,
Both in the soil and in your deeds.

Nurture passions, let them grow,
In this lunar, fertile glow.

Blossom forth, embrace the chance,
To let your spirit truly dance.

With each flower that blooms anew,
May's *Flower Moon* blesses you.

Embrace the fecund power it sends,
And watch with joy as your spirit transcends.

24
Today I sent an encouraging card,
To a friend who is finding life hard.

I'm hoping that when it lands on her mat,
The gathering gloom it will help her combat.

For I love it when I get mail that isn't a bill,
Or a statement of how much was rung up at the till.

My mag subscription can make me smile,
With tips on how to adopt the latest style.

A postcard from some sunny spot,
Can cheer me up quite a lot.

So whilst it may seem old-fashioned to craft a letter,
Send one today—you'll make someone's day better.

25
My friend loves Yoga; I prefer Tai Chi.
Which better suits the essence of me.

In every move, in every stance,
Tai Chi's rhythm is my dance.

It helps you deal with stress and go with the flow.
By doing it, the seeds of serenity you will sow.

Embrace Tiger; *Return to Mountain*:
Health flows through one like a gentle fountain.

With *Grasp Bird's Tail* and *Cloud Hands*, too,
You will find balance and your strength renew.

Health and harmony will come your way.
With Tai Chi's positivity, you'll greet the day.

26

I wanted to bring my hard-working hubby some cheer,
So I took him off to a festival of beer.

I knew that in lifting his spirits it wouldn't fail,
When he saw those many casks of real ale.

As he sampled one or two,
What was a fizz girl like me to do?

Well, luckily for me, there stood a stall,
That shone like a beacon amidst them all.

Yes, amongst beers and ales of every variety,
Someone had kindly thought of me.

Prosecco was on offer, my heart gave a cheer.
We had a great time, and I was Wife of the Year!

27

What is the point of the pigeon?
I ask myself when awoken each day by their din.

If I put food out for another bird,
They steal it, and they can look tatty and quite absurd.

Wait, though, to appreciate all creation, I know I should,
So let's contemplate the things about the pigeon that are good:

Carrying messages, they helped us win the war.
A home run back to their coop they brilliantly score.

The thing, though, about the pigeon that is the best:
Look closely; they have a beautiful rainbow on their chest.

So it seems this pesky bird has become my teacher,
That there is wonder to be found in the most humble creature.

28

I love cheese,
It never fails to please.

Mozzarella on my pizza, melted just right;
Parmesan on pasta, a savoury delight.

Swiss with its holes, so fun to eat;
Camembert smooth, oh, what a treat!

Feta in my salad, tangy and bright;
Gruyère in fondue, on a warm, cosy night.

Cheddar in my sandwich, with chutney every time;
Halloumi, grilled, transports me to a sunnier clime.

Of cheese, I can never ever get my fill;
I love it so—lunch, dinner, snack—it always fits the bill.

29

Do you have a power song?
One that can help make your world right when it all seems wrong?

A song that takes you forward when you're behind,
Or persuades to change your mind?

One that can make you feel confident,
And help you achieve an accomplishment

Mine is Katy Perry's *Firework*:
It defeats my self-doubt and dispels the murk.

If you don't have a power song, may I suggest you choose,
One that you can always use.

For whenever you need a helping hand,
Using it's power, a bullseye you will always land.

30

In the town of Quirkyville, the businesses delight,
With names that make you chuckle, from morning until night.

There's *A Cut Above*, the hairdressers, where style's always grand,
They snip and clip with flair, the best in all the land.

Down by the seaside, *The Cod Father* reigns supreme,
With fish and chips so tasty, they're the stuff of dreams.

The shop next door, *Brewed Awakening*, where coffee's strong and fine,
A morning cup from here will truly make you shine.

For sweet treats and pastries, try *Bake My Day* for sure,
Their cakes and cookies scrumptious, you'll be coming back for more.

The Grill Sergeant serves BBQ that's smoked just right,
With flavours bold and smoky, it's a carnivore's delight.

Need a book or two to read? *Once Upon a Spine* is great,
A book store full of stories that you simply can't negate.

And for a sparkling clean, it's *Grime and Punishment*,
The best in town for washing, their service Heaven-sent.

Pet Pawlor pampers pets with care so fine,
From fur to claw, they're groomed so they simply shine.

So if you visit Quirkyville, explore these shops so grand,
With names that bring a smile, they're the best in all the land.

Each business has its charm, a unique and clever name,
In the heart of Quirkyville, no two are quite the same.

31

I love plants, trees and flowers,
But I don't like getting grubby, or putting in the hours.

Gardening is simply not my cup of tea.
But I'd like to thank all those who make nice spaces for me.

There's a lovely green park near where I live,
It's been created by those who give,

Of their time to tend it well,
Lovingly caring for rose and bluebell.

When I sit there, it never fails to give a lift;
To me, it is a heavenly gift,

From those who don't mind getting mucky,
Whose work enhances my life, making me lucky,

That I can enjoy the beauty they have grown.
My joy has blossomed in their work and the seeds they have sown.

June

1

On National Bubbly Day, let's raise a toast,
To celebrate with fizz—the wine I love most.

I'm known as the Bubbly Girl, for I adore sparkling wine:
Prosecco, Champagne, Cava—O! those bubbles so divine!

In celebrations grand, and moments pure and sweet,
Wine with bubbles brings us joy and makes the day complete.

Today, because it's Saturday, is the perfect time
To invite your friends and celebrate with bubbles so sublime.

Pop the Prosecco, pour the Cava, let Champagne flow with cheer,
Delightful fruity flavours in every glass appear.

National Bubbly Day, always a weekend's bliss,
Enjoy it without the worry of Monday's work abyss.

In this bubbly celebration, let happiness abide.
Me? I'll raise my glass and own my name: the Bubbly Girl, with pride.

2

In night's quiet, when the world is still,
Waking can cause one's soul to chill.

Thoughts turn dark like the shadows, deep,
Drawing you further from dreamy sleep.

Doubts creep in and love seems far,
Underneath the midnight star.

Questions rise, answers flee,
Nothing's clear in that late-night sea.

Hold fast until morning's light;
When dawn breaks, things turn bright.

As Aurora ushers in a new dawn, hope is made;
Miraculously, worries fade,

So remember, in the darkest hour,
Just wait to feel the morning's power.

For though night may doom foretell,
Trust, come morning, all will be well.

3

Today I have lots to do,
Including writing a rhyme for you.

So here's the challenge: can I produce a rhyme,
That makes sense in double-quick time?

They say that stress can motivate,
Provoking a performance that can be great.

Can that be true in the world of the poet?
I think it can—in fact, I know it.

In minutes, I've managed to produce this little ditty,
I hope you find it engaging and perhaps quite witty.

4

Of rugby I have never been a fan,
But, of Rob Burrow, I was—such an amazing man.

Always a team player, when he got MND,
He took to his heart the whole community.

Rob never gave up or bemoaned his lot,
To fundraise for the cause, he gave all he had got.

Supported by his friend Kev and wife Lindsey,
Rob became an inspiration for all to see.

So as we wish this hero a fond goodbye,
Let's salute him for his final brilliant try,

Not on the field, but in his life,
Excelling to the end through pain and strife.

5

I've got a device that's all the rage.
It's supposed to help me as I age.

It shines light upon my face;
When I wear it, in a sci-fi movie, I wouldn't look out of place.

Though with the lines, it will help, I hope.
Of course, it is limited in its scope.

To my physical being; it doesn't help my heart,
Which I'd like to think is my loveliest part.

For what is it that really makes my face shine?
Birdsong in the morning and a text from a friend of mine.

A good dance, a good laugh—these are always a gift.
With these to make me smile, maybe I don't need no facelift.

6

Cows get a bad press, some people just see,
The methane they produce naturally.

But there's more to a cow than just gas, don't you know?
They teach us to be content and to let our worries go.

Out in the fields, they chew the cud with ease,
Giving us milk and delightful cheese.

Two of my favourite things which bring comfort and balm,
From the cows who graze and do no harm.

In some lovely farms, you can cuddle a cow,
For therapy, to stay calm & just be— they'll show you how.

Reducing anxiety, bringing peace so profound,
With a cow by your side, tranquillity's found.

So let's give cows a break and change the narrative,
From methane talk to live and let live.

For they teach us to just to rest and be.
That's a profound lesson for you and me.

7

I must admit I love a quote.
I get inspired by words other people said, or wrote.

Why fit in when you were born to stand out?,
That fits the bill for me, no doubt.

Tomorrow is another day,
Helps me when lots of crap is thrown my way.

The one, though, that never fails to fill my spiritual cup,
Is, *It's not how many times you fall, but how many times you get up.*

I'd like to think that, one day, someone my words will read,
When they are in a time of need.

That my words might help them is a lovely thought.
Here's one from me: *It is your own approval that should be sought.*

Yes, words are powerful, so let's use them well,
For in doing so, you may encourage or comfort— you never can tell.

8

In springtime's gentle, warming, light,
The mayflies dance, a fleeting sight.

From depths of water they arise,
To greet the world with eager eyes.

For males, two days are all they own,
While females live mere minutes alone.

Yet in their brief, bright, span of day,
They mate; they shine; then fade away.

They gather around the glowing light,
To mate and savour their short flight.

For 350 million years they've flown,
A message in their dance is shown.

Their story whispers in our ear,
A powerful lesson, bright and clear:

Seize the day; don't let it pass,
Without making every moment last.

As we emerge from winter's shade
And step into the springtime glade,

Just like the mayfly, let us strive,
To live our best while we're alive.

9

We've just bought a house, and it's got a room with a view.
It's in my husband's study and will help him look anew,

At the world when it is getting him down,
When his work pressures make him stress and frown.

It will help him remember that there is more to life,
Than endless stress, toil, and strife.

As he looks out and sees endless green,
Between Zoom calls and a dull routine,

I'm glad he's got a view; he deserves it so,
For he works harder than any man I know.

May he look across those fields and realise,
That I wish nothing less for him than the bluest of skies.

10

In life, we all have our unique taste;
One's joy is another's time to waste.

I hate to cook, but love to dine;
A good meal makes everything fine.

Cleaning's a chore, that much is true,
But a tidy house I love to view.

Gardening, oh, not my delight,
Yet a lovely space makes my world seem bright.

Shopping. for me, is never a chore:
I love to hunt bargains in every store.

Managing money, I keep the accounts in a row;
It keeps us secure, makes our wealth grow.

Shredding documents is a task I adore;
Ensuring our safety, it's never a bore.

Together we function, at some skill we ace;
In the grand puzzle of life, we find our place.

We're all unique, like pieces in a game,
Each one essential, none the same.

Though we're all different, it's plain to see,
Our unity is our strength, so let's live and let others be.

11

By a tranquil canal, my home does rest,
A lovely part of the world; I am truly blessed.

But deep in my soul, a yearning does grow,
For the rush of the river and its steady flow.

As a Cancerian, water calls my name.
It's in my nature, and it's always been the same.

The flowing water cleanses my soul,
Washing away emotions, making me whole.

The river's journey, relentless and free,
Carries my burdens far away from me.

Though I cherish the canal and its peaceful grace,
Every now and then, I seek a new place.

To the sea or a river, I must sometimes flee,
To feel refreshed and truly be me.

12

Carers week, a time to acknowledge the kindness and care,
Given by those who are always there.

Through sleepless nights and busy days,
They show their love in so many ways.

Through every challenge, great and small,
Carers answer every call.

They give their strength, they share their cheer,
Wiping away each worry and tear.

Unsung heroes in life's challenging tale,
Their spirits strong, they never fail.

So here's to carers, with gratitude deep,
For the promises they faithfully keep.

During National Carers Week, we honour you,
For all the amazing things you do.

13

This morning started with a crash—what a mess!
My coffee pot shattered which caused distress.

Coffee dreams lay broken, scattered on the floor,
So out came the vacuum, a task I abhor.

Grumbling and mumbling, I cleaned up the spill,
Wishing for calm, instead of this ill.

But I paused for a moment, took a breath along the way,
Decided this mishap won't determine the rest of my day.

A shift in my mood, a change in my view,
This small morning mishap, I'd bid it adieu.

For the day's still ahead, with wonders to see,
Magic and miracles, waiting for me.

Attitude is key, to what lies in store,
So I chose to embrace what the day had, and more.

So here's to the day, with its ups and its downs,
With laughter and joy, more smiles than frowns.

For one small thing won't darken my light,
I'll l seek out the magic from morning to night.

14

There's a saying: *Treat each day as if it's your last*,
But how about a twist- a different contrast?

Imagine every morning, the world brand new,
Seeing it all for the first time, in every hue.

The sight of a flower, delicate and bright,
A miracle of colour, a pure delight.

Your loved one's face, as warm as the sunrise,
The look of acceptance in your friend's eyes.

A bird in flight, graceful and free,
A tree's grand stature, a marvel to see.

A waterfall cascading, a silver dance,
Each drop a wonder, a joyful trance.

Sipping coffee, that first taste sublime,
A moment to savour and take your time.

A fresh outlook on all that you do,
Rediscovering joys, finding the new.

Imagine each day as if it were your first,
See the world afresh, let your heart burst.

15

Skipton is such a gorgeous little town,
However, the weather can sometimes get me down.

For there's a price to be paid for all this green:
So much rain in all my days I have never seen.

Today, as soon as I left my door,
The heavens opened and it began to pour.

Out came my trusted brolly.
Off I went to the supermarket to fill my trolley.

Alas, once finished, my brolly was nowhere in sight.
I searched and searched with all my might.

Eventually, I was helped by a customer service lady,
Who had a lovely surprise for me.

Someone had handed in my brolly; it was there.
I was so grateful that someone had bothered to care.

I gave thanks for the friendliness of this town of mine.
Yes, it rains in Skipton, but together we create our own sunshine.

16

On Father's Day, I remember well,
A man of strength, with tales to tell.

Desmond, my father, worked the mines,
Deep in the pit, where no sun shines.

He called me his bairn, with a love so true,
When college came, it hurt us both to bid adieu.

Dropped me off, with great hopes for me, his chum,
Found an acorn, kept as a symbol of what I could become.

During the strike, he kept his fire cold,
Paid my grant, his warmth on hold.

Each visit I'd make, he'd wave with such cheer,
The last time I turned, I shed a sad tear.

For I knew in my heart, it was our final farewell,
Yet his spirit remains, in memories I dwell.

He loved cricket and Scarborough's sea,
I picture him there, watching happily.

One day I'll join him, with fish and chips in hand,
We'll sit and snuggle, on Scarborough's sand.

For now, I cherish these memories true,
On Father's Day, Dad, I'm thinking of you.

17

In poetry, as in life, challenges abound.
Today's: can I end each line with the same sound?

Life is easier, I have found,
When you have fun, so I will just mess around,

With words and hope my try doesn't rebound,
And that my efforts will find fertile ground,

Making you smile, hoping you haven't frowned.
Then the *Queen of Rhyming*, I will be crowned.

18

In the morning light, toast so warm,
A scent that banishes the gloomiest storm.

Coffee brews, rich and bold,
A liquid hug when the world is cold.

Roses in bloom, so sweet and bright,
Their fragrance a joy—pure delight.

Lavender fields in a gentle breeze,
Calm the soul and put one's mind at ease.

Baby powder soft, a gentle embrace,
A scent that brings a smile to my face.

My husband's skin, so warm, so near,
The scent of love I hold most dear.

These scents, they weave a perfect tale
Of life's small joys that never pale.

19

Approaching 60 can be hard.
Am I fit for the knacker's yard?

Or are there adventures still to be had,
People and things to make my heart glad?

Some people never see 60; they have no choice,
So upon reaching this milestone, I should rejoice,

That I have been given the privilege of life.
Count my successes; I'm a brilliant chum and a lovely wife.

Look forward to the future with a grateful heart.
Yes, 60 ain't so bad—pour the fizz, let the fun start.

20

O radiant Sun, with golden might,
On Solstice day, we seek your light.

Grant us strength and harmony,
As we bask in your majesty.

With golden rays, our spirits lift,
Your warmth a most cherished gift,

Of your power we never tire,
Ignite our dreams, take us higher,

Bless our days with joy and cheer,
As we celebrate the turning of the year,

Your brilliance guiding us ever near,
Chasing shadows and calming fear.

With strength and joy, our days imbued,
Our dreams alight, our hopes renewed.

In gratitude, our voices raise,
To you, O Sun, our songs of praise.

21

Tonight, will rise the full *Strawberry Moon*,
Gracing the skies of flaming June.

In mid-summer, shining full and bright,
Lightening the dark with ivory light.

In North America, it's a sign,
That strawberries ripen on the vine.

Algonquin tribes knew well this treat,
The full *Strawberry Moon* meant a seasonal beat.

But, in Europe, the moon's allure
Is known by names that still endure:

The *Honey Moon*, a term so sweet,
Signifies love, romance, a treat.

Newly-weds would celebrate,
With mead and honey, sealing their romantic fate.

The full moon marks the fullest bliss,
A symbol of a wedding kiss.

Also known as *Hot* or *Hay*,
For summer's start and harvest's day.

So when the full moon does appear,
Cherish the things, or folk, you hold dear.

This evening please enjoy this wondrous sight,
A gift from the Cosmos, it will entrance and delight.

22

Happy Birthday to you, dear Cancer Moon Child,
With a heart so warm and a spirit so mild.

Your loyalty shines like the light of the moon,
You nurture and care, like a sweet, gentle tune.

Intuitive and deep, you feel with your soul,
In your comforting presence, we all feel whole.

Your creativity blooms like a garden in spring,
You're thoughtful and kind, such joy you bring.

Sometimes you're moody, like the tide's restless flow.
Too sensitive, sometimes, but that helps you grow.

You can be clingy, and retreat into your shell,
Yet your love and support always cast a magic spell.

So celebrate today, let your heart be light,
With Tom Hanks and Margot Robbie, your stars shine bright.

For you share your sign with them, and with me too,
Happy Birthday, dear Cancerian, the world adores you!

23

What is your favourite film and what does it say about you?
I can't pick just one or even two.

Each film that I love, reveals something about me,
So let's take a journey, then more of me you'll see.

Starting with *The Wizard of Oz*, the search for the rainbow's end,
Filled me with hope when little and I needed a friend.

Dirty Dancing showed me that even an insecure girl,
Can take to the floor and give life a spectacular twirl.

As Good as It Gets taught that even in vulnerability,
I could find love and people to care for me.

Finally, I love Christmas, so *Jingle All the Way*,
A tale of how even someone flawed can save the day.

Those are mine; please review with an open heart.
Tell me yours and perhaps a lovely friendship we can start.

24

In the game of life, we all play our role,
Sometimes we shoot for the stars, striving to reach a goal.

When things get tough and we feel we've had enough,
Knocked for six, we feel life is too rough.

But before you call it quits, take a time-out,
Regroup your thoughts, banish the doubt.

If you feel offside, stay true to your heart,
With a strong game plan, you'll be ready to start.

It's not my forte, we might say,
When tough times come our way.

But with courage, strong and hard,
We face each test, no holds barred.

You'll face many hurdles, but you can still ace,
For life is a marathon; it's not just a race.

Whether you're in the final inning or the first quarter play,
Keep pushing forward, come what may.

So don't throw in the towel, keep your head in the game,
With perseverance and passion, there's much more to gain.

In the end, it's our spirit, our drive to strive,
That makes us champions in this journey of life.

25

In a *Yellow Submarine*, let's set out and explore,
The magic of The Beatles, from days of yore.

On *The Long and Winding Road*, as we travel far and wide,
Their melodies and harmonies in our hearts reside.

Through trials and troubles, in times of woe,
They whispered the wisdom to *Let It Be* so.

From *Yesterday* to *Help!*, the tunes we adore,
Melodies I will cherish *When I'm Sixty-Four*.

Their songs still echo, in hearts and in minds,
As a group, they were one of a kind.

So here's to The Beatles, their legacy grand,
Their songs bring us joy, a timeless band.

With guitars, drums and harmonies that fit like a glove,
They showed us, forever, that *All You Need Is Love*.

26

If you really are what you eat,
That makes me very sweet.

You see, my favourite food is cake;
In a buffet, the salad I would never take.

My friend loves nothing more than coconut,
If the principle applies, she'd be happy in a beach hut.

As for my hubby, he adores a slice of bread;
To me, he's indispensable, it has to be said.

Maybe one day I will come to love caviar;
Would that make me a superstar?

So if we really are what we eat, let's rejoice,
In our every unique food choice,

And not treat food as a chore:
Oatcakes and cider vinegar, oh, what a bore.

27

In the early morning, I'm up with a spark,
Bright and cheerful, I'm known as the lark.

The sun's just rising, the world starts to glow,
I love the fresh start, the early bird show.

I sip my coffee as the day breaks anew,
The quiet of dawn brings a peaceful view.

I get things done while the world is still,
The morning calm gives me such a thrill.

But my friend, the owl, stays up late at night,
When the stars are out, her world feels right.

In the quiet dark, creativity flows,
A different kind of peace, that's how it goes.

They find their magic under moon's soft gleam,
The stillness of night fuels their dream.

While I am asleep, they work with might,
For owls, the night is the time that's bright.

Being a lark means I seize the day,
The early hours are where I play.

I find my rhythm with the rising sun,
A fresh new start before the day's begun.

Being an owl means they own the dark,
As on journeys within they embark.

Their ideas flourish when the world is still,
Their nighttime hours bring a special thrill.

Larks greet the dawn with energy and grace,
Owls find their peace in the nighttime space.

Both have their strengths, both have their cheer,
Together we seize the whole day, that's clear.

28

It is well to have as many holds upon happiness as possible, Jane Austen wrote.
What could she have meant, this woman of note?

Don't make one person, or thing, the reason for your joy;
Change is inevitable, so we need to deploy,

A strategy to see us through,
When tough times come, as they always do.

Instead of relying on one relationship which could end,
Make sure you cultivate more than one friend.

If you have a venue that you think is ace,
A restaurant, or pub, maybe find a different place.

Perhaps the thing that lifts you is a special brew;
Why not try a new blend ,or two?

In life, things, or people can be taken away,
But with our happiness backup plan, we can save our own day.

29

We all have a temperature that we think is ideal.
If it gets above 18 degrees, overwhelmed is how I feel.

I think perhaps it's in my DNA;
Hailing from the North, searing heat just ain't my way.

My friend, on the other hand, loves the heat.
For her, a scorching day just can't be beat.

So I guess when it comes to the sun,
There just ain't no pleasing everyone.

As I wave at my basking friend from the shade,
I remember we're all unique; it's just how we're made.

30

Aujourd'hui je tente de rimer en français,
Avec des mots doux, s'il vous plaît.

Je cherche l'inspiration dans chaque coin,
Pour que mes rimes soient fines et sans foin.

Chaque ligne, je peaufine sans cesse,
Pour que mes rimes soient une vraie prouesse.

Rimer en français, c'est un beau défi,
Mais je m'y applique avec grand souci.

July

1

At halfway through this year we stand,
A time to pause and look back on all we'd planned.

Reflect on all the trails we beat,
Every win and every defeat.

In the middle, things might seem unclear,
But don't give in to doubt or fear.

The year's not done, there's time to grow,
For all our dreams to start to show.

Celebrate the victories, big or small,
Each one a step, each one a call.

To keep on pushing, through the fray,
Imagine how you'll feel that day.

When December comes, and you look back,
At all you've done to stay on track.

So here's to us, to hope and cheer,
Let's make the most of our remaining year.

2

There's a crystal I'd like to recommend to you,
It's Amethyst; in life, it can be a friend so true.

It heals the mind with gentle ease,
Easing worries, bringing peace.

In troubled times, it's your guide,
A calming force by your side.

For the body, it's a soothing balm,
Easing tension, restoring calm.

Amethyst wards off pain, brings restful sleep,
In its presence, no fears creep.

For clarity, it lights the way,
Banishes confusion, keeps stress at bay.

It mends the spirit, heals the soul,
With Amethyst, you become whole.

So cherish this crystal, purple and bright,
A soothing presence, a beacon of light.

Mind, body, soul, all aligned,
In Amethyst's embrace, true peace you'll find.

3

I'm a minimal effort, maximum results, kind of gal,
So when I need a boost, I listen to a subliminal.

Subliminals are music that contain a message within;
At the game of life, they can help you win.

You select a piece of music to play,
Then let its hidden affirmations alter your day.

They can transform for the better your state of mind,
Give you a confidence boost, or help you unwind.

So next time you feel life getting too much,
Let a subliminal soothe you with its loving touch.

4

At the heart of the country, there's a charity so kind,
Parkinson's UK, with a mission designed,

To offer advice and information so clear,
Campaigning for justice, helping defeat fear.

Tirelessly, they research and support,
For those with Parkinson's, they're a comforting port.

To help those affected, we can do our part,
With tolerance and patience, right from the heart.

Michael J. Fox, a beacon so bold,
Just one of the warriors with spirits of gold.

Their inner being shines, undeterred by disease,
Smiling still, though life ain't no breeze.

Parkinson's UK stands by their side,
With love and care, a kindly guide.

So let's join the fight, let's lend a hand,
Together we can make a stand.

For Parkinson's UK, let's give some time,
For the road is long, but with hope, the mountain we will climb.

5

As I sat, relaxing, just the other day,
A joyful sound came my way.

The tune was nostalgic; it took me back,
It was the ice cream van; I just fancied a naughty snack.

Filled with joy, I dashed outside,
To support the seller, my calorie counter I denied.

I asked for a 99, my favourite treat.
Three pounds, he said; my heart skipped a nervous beat.

Alone at the van, I couldn't decline,
I took the cone; an expensive but lovely prize was mine.

O! What a let-down, the ice cream so bland,
The flake wasn't authentic, not what I'd planned.

No more will I visit that disappointing van.
To the supermarket I'll go; that's my new plan.

My inner child will pine for days gone by,
While the passing of innocence I decry.

6

Today, I want to talk to you on the subject of the loo,
Don't worry I won't dwell too much on the subject of wee and poo.

I simply want to protest at the lack of public loos,
Which is very inconvenient and leaves me with the blues.

When you want to spend a penny, what a chore it is to face:
You have to throw yourself on the mercy of a cafe or a pub's grace.

Another bugbear of mine is the Unisex loo,
When I'm attending to my makeup, I don't want a man in view.

I love men and trust most of them, there's no doubt,
But there are some bad eggs, and it gives me a bout,

Of worry for my safety, when I just want some space,
To adjust my outfit and feel secure in the place.

So here's my little rhyme on the matter of the loo,
Let's hope for more public options, convenient and new.

And maybe separate spaces for privacy's sake,
For a more comfortable visit, that's the change we should make.

7

Always *Shine* your light, clear and bright,
Be the star that illuminates the darkest night.

Let each day be your *Greatest Day*.
With *Patience* you will find a way.

Never Forget the dreams you chase,
It Only Takes a Minute to put a smile on your face.

You can *Rule the World* if you take a chance,
Get your hope *Back for Good* and join life's dance.

For life's a song to be sung, and sung loud!
With Take That's words, live strong, live proud!

8

On Saturday night, on the sofa with my man,
Watching the footie, though I'm not a true fan.

It was the end of the game and I was captivated.
The game left me feeling elated.

Five brave men ready to battle with fate,
Illustrating all that is great,

About the human spirit, when faced with a task,
That seems too much to ask.

Each player fought hard for the England team,
Doing their utmost to bring home a dream.

As the five goals went in, I learned such a lot:
That sometimes life takes all we've got;

But if we move forward with faith in our heart,
We will set ourselves apart,

From those who let fear rule their life,
Who buckle at the sign of any strife.

So well done, lads, I salute you all,
And remember, on Wednesday, keep your eye on the ball.

9

Magenta, oh, how you shine so bright,
A favourite colour, a pure delight.

A blend of red and blue, so true,
Masculine and feminine, in perfect hue.

In colour therapy, you hold such might,
Balancing energies, making everything right.

You bring compassion, uplift the heart,
With your presence, healing can start.

In our clothes, you make a bold statement,
In home decor, you're pure enchantment.

From cushions to curtains, or even a wall,
Magenta's touch can transform it all.

In gardens, you bloom with vibrant cheer,
Flowers of magenta bring joy near.

So let this colour into your life,
To soothe the soul and ease the strife.

10

One of the advantages of being married to a younger man,
Is that he shares with me the TV shows of which he was a fan.

In his younger years, TV that passed by me,
Whilst I was away studying for my degree.

He's introduced me to *The Golden Girls*, a great show
That, to me, deals ageism a terrific blow.

It illustrates women who are brave and strong,
Witty and bright, in later life finding the place where they belong.

When, for love and understanding, these ladies yearn,
It's to their tight friendship group that they turn.

So, thanks to my hubby for giving me this gift:
'The Golden Girls', always insightful, always gives my mood a lift.

11

My apologies to you today; I just don't have the time,
To spend on writing you even a little rhyme.

You see, I have a big list of things to do,
So why would I waste time rhyming for you?

Hmm, perhaps there's another way to look at this.
If I didn't rhyme for you, it's something I would really miss.

And surely one of the best parts of me,
Is my quirky creativity.

So it's clear that I need to open my eyes,
Get my shit together, and prioritise.

You, who have done me the honour of visiting X each day,
Shown me that it's important to have fun and play.

For *The way we spend our time defines who we are*,
So it's goodbye, and thank you, from this Cosmic Rhyming Superstar.

Quote by: Jonathan Estrin

12

When chaos swirls and steals your peace,
Remember the breath of life can bring release.

Take a breath, slow and deep,
Feel the calm begin to seep.

Breathing anchors you to the now,
If you want to know how:

Tai Chi encourages mindful flow,
Teaching you how to breathe just so.

Meditation's quiet art,
Centres mind and calms the heart.

Focus on the breath—be here,
Letting go of doubt and fear.

When life's a storm, a wild ride,
Breathing's there, a friend beside.

The breath of life, so pure and true,
Can bring you back, renew, redo.

So take a breath when times are tough,
In through the nose, let out the rough.

With every breath, find your ground,
Peace and clarity can be found.

13

In days of joy and skies so bright,
I admire those who keep in sight,

How lucky they are to bask in the light;
Their praise of the Divine feels right.

When troubles knock on our door,
Many pray who've not before.

It's easy to seek a higher might
When facing shadows in the night.

Yet, when the sun shines every day
And all our worries fade away,

How rare it is for us to pause and say,
Thank you for our vista being blue, not grey.

So let's take a moment, a humble plea,
To honour whatever for us the Divine might be.

In joy and sorrow, let's agree
To let gratitude flow eternally.

14

Would three lions beat a bull in a fight?
Well, I think perhaps they just might.

And, tonight, as England take on Spain,
I believe a decisive victory they will gain.

England may have got off to a slow start,
But now they're playing from the heart.

Expertly led by Gareth Southgate,
Much maligned; now acknowledged as great.

So it is abundantly clear,
Football's Coming Home is the chant we'll hear!

15

Peacock, Blue, or Cabbage White,
Butterflies are such a lovely sight.

To see one, I am always keen;
This year, though, so few have I seen.

But this year, rain has soaked the sky;
None of them have buzzed on by.

The garden's still, the flowers wait,
For visitors who come too late.

I miss the hum of bees and butterflies so bright,
A summer chorus out of sight.

I wouldn't greet a wasp with cheer,
But now their absence feels so queer.

These tiny signs of summer days
Have vanished in the rainfall's haze.

I hope they're safe, in some retreat,
Waiting for the sun to greet.

May they return, bee and butterfly,
To dance beneath a clear blue sky.

16

Every day, I enter with glee,
Competitions, always for free.

I send each entry; in my heart, there's hope.
With the drudge of life, it helps me cope.

It's a joy that makes my world a little brighter,
Each chance a spark, making my days lighter.

I've won clothes, a TV, and a mini break,
These gifts and joys, I gladly take.

Even if I never won a single prize,
My life's treasures are in front of my eyes.

A lovely husband, my heart's true delight;
Good friends, who make my days so right.

A gorgeous town, where dreams come true:
I'm blessed and lucky in all that I do.

So I'll keep on entering, with hopeful cheer,
Grateful for my luck, year after year.

17

Happy Birthday today to me, the Cosmic Rhymer.
At 60, does this mean I'm now viewed as an old-timer?

I hope not, 'cause in life, I had a rocky start.
It took me years to heal my heart.

It was in my 30s that I conquered strife,
And claim my space as a warrior of life.

Nowadays, I cut myself some slack,
Allow myself to turn the clock back.

For, to me, life has just got going,
All my guns are blazing, my creativity's flowing.

So join me, today, in my 30th (!) birthday celebration.
May it be filled with cake, bubbles, and elation!

18

In days of old, Latin thrived,
Of this ancient language, words have survived.

From ancient Rome to modern times,
Phrases are still used, even in rhymes.

Carpe diem—seize the day,
Make the most of it in every way.

Status quo—let things rest,
Resist the change, not always advice that's best.

Et cetera—and so it goes,
A list that ends, yet still flows.

Bona fide—true and pure,
A promise kept, intentions sure.

Vice versa—switch around,
In reverse, the opposite found.

Alibi—where were you?
A tale to tell, a truth to view.

Mea culpa—my mistake,
A fault confessed, for peace's sake.

From Rome to now, these words still abound,
In our lives their wisdom can be found.

19

On International Karaoke Day, let's all give a cheer out loud,
My voice is awful, but I still have fun joining the crowd.

In Manchester's bars, I found my own flair,
Dancing to Bon Jovi's *Living on a Prayer*.

Though my voice might not charm, my moves stole the show,
As I grooved to the rhythm, feeling the glow.

As it's Friday today the time is just right,
To head to a Karaoke bar and sing through the night.

Karaoke's a joy, with benefits in store,
It's good for the soul and we should do it more.

A great stress reliever, it brightens our day,
Evoking community, as strangers cheer us on our way.

So grab the mic, and let your spirit shine bright,
Join the fun and sing your heart, don't dim your light.

Whether you're a singer or prefer to dance,
Karaoke's magic gives everyone a chance.

20

Weary after doing my big supermarket shop,
Awaiting my taxi, onto a bench I flop.

When out of the corner of my eye,
I spotted a very interesting guy.

By the look of him, he had lived quite a life,
Seen his share of pleasure and strife.

So, rather than staying in my own space,
I decided to give this stranger a little place,

In my day to listen to the tales he had to tell,
And the brief time we spent together was quite swell.

He educated me on my town's history,
Spinning yarns of how it used to be.

My taxi came; I waved goodbye.
Today's lesson: reach out, connect—go on, just try.

Then your world will expand,
For in this journey, we're stronger walking hand in hand.

21

If you were a biscuit, what kind would you be?
A crisp, crunchy treat, or a dunker for tea?

Maybe a Ginger Snap with a spicy zing,
Or a Rich Tea that's classic, no fuss, no bling?

Are you like a Hobnob, sturdy and tough,
Weathering life's storms, not dissolving when things get rough?

Or perhaps a Digestive, sweet yet plain,
Steady and reliable, never causing strain?

Could you be a Shortbread, buttery and rich,
A comforting friend when life hits a glitch?

Or a Bourbon, oh so suave and sleek,
With a hidden depth, far from meek?

I'd be a Jammy Dodger, you see,
Hard on the outside, but that's not all of me.

For within my core, there's a squishy part:
A soft, sweet jam—that's my tender heart.

22

Though born in the heart of midsummer's blaze,
I confess, I don't bask in its sunlit haze.

The heat is too much; it's hard to endure,
Which clothes to choose, I'm never quite sure.

In summer, there's pressure to always be out,
But the sweltering heat makes me want to shout.

I long for the cold, for winter's embrace,
Where staying at home is no fall from grace.

In winter, I find a snug, cosy, delight,
In warm, comfy, clothes, holding loved ones tight.

No guilt in staying where it's cosy and warm,
Protected from snow and the wild winter storm.

This year, though, even I have longed for the sun,
For we all need some when all's said and done.

So, with everyone else, in its presence I will rejoice:
Yes, please stay a while, Mr. Sun—that's my unexpected choice!

23

Happy Birthday, dear Leo, today's your day to shine bright,
Born in summer's warmth and golden light.

With a heart full of courage and a spirit full of joy,
You possess an optimism no care can destroy.

You're loyal and kind, with a generous soul,
A leader at heart, taking charge is your goal.

Your creativity sparkles, your confidence glows,
In every endeavour, your brilliance shows.

With passion fierce, you light the way,
Your charm and grace in full display.

Creative souls with visions grand,
You lead us all with a guiding hand.

Sometimes stubborn, prideful too,
Impatient, fiery, through and through.

But even with your flaws in view,
We love the star that is you.

Madonna shares your sign, a woman we adore.
Chris Hemsworth too, also known as Thor!

And my friend Emma, warrior, goddess true,
This day belongs to all of you.

So happy birthday, Leos dear,
May joy and love be always near.

In your majestic, roaring style,
Your gift to the world is to make us smile.

24

Even in summer, the world can seem grey,
So, today, we honour Samaritans Awareness Day.

If in the darkest tunnel, they are a light at the end,
Helping by being a selfless friend.

When hope seems lost and fears abound,
A Samaritan's voice is a calming sound.

In times of need, when spirits tire,
They stoke the flames of our inner fire.

With empathy and care so true,
They help us to start our lives anew.

To each who gives to their time and love,
You're a blessing sent from up above.

Thank you, dear friends, for the hope that you give,
For your caring and support, helping others to live.

25

I'm a Baby Boomer. Gen Z,
Seems to have a different language to me,

One you may find hard to understand,
But I'm here to translate and hold your hand.

When they say *Drip*, they're talking about style,
A flashy outfit that makes 'em smile.

Slay means they're winning, doing their best,
Crushing the game, passing every test.

Vibing is chillin', just feeling good,
Enjoying the moment, as everyone should.

If they're feeling *Salty*, they're mad or upset,
Not in a good mood, feeling some regret.

And *Fam* means family, not just by blood,
Close friends and loved ones, through bad times and good.

Having written this poem, I don't mean to gloat,
But in Gen Z parlance, I think it's the *GOAT*!

26

I love the experience of afternoon tea,
A chance to indulge and dress in my finery.

In lovely surroundings, for an hour or two,
You can forget that list of things to do.

Be waited on with a smile,
Imagine you're posh, just for a while.

So tomorrow, I will meet a mate,
And visit a hotel we know is great.

Get the bubbles flowing and eat our fill;
Yes, I adore afternoon tea and always will.

27

Happy Birthday to me, once again,
Twice the joy and double the gain.

First with my husband, a lovely day,
Cards and gifts, feeling blessed in every way.

Then with my dear friend, such fun.
Prosecco and R&R, both hard-won.

Delicious food we'll savour in moments so pleasant,
She'll spoil me with gifts, each one a true present.

Gifts galore, laughter so bright,
Two birthdays for my heart, a double delight.

Here's to the Queen, who set the trend,
Two birthdays, happiness without end.

Cheers to me, let's raise a toast,
To the people I love; they're the gifts I cherish most!

28

I've never been known to hug a tree,
But that doesn't mean they don't mean the world to me.

I have memories from when I was very small,
Of running under willow trees, not so tall.

Big enough, though, to provide shade and shelter,
When the day's heat made me swelter.

At other times, when I needed to find peace,
Gazing on trees helped me find release.

When experiencing turmoil and strife,
Trees' green bounty calmed my life.

So today, let's take a brief moment,
To thank these beauties which were Heaven-sent.

29

Hello, dear reader! Just under a year ago,
I promised to rhyme each day and let my creative juices flow.

Sometimes to make you think, or to bring you laughter,
But I didn't bank on the morning after.

I can't lie to you and pretend I'm in clover,
When I've got a teensy-weensy hangover.

Today, it's really hard for me to think,
When laid low by the effects of drink.

This isn't something of which I'm proud;
However, I'd like to state this out loud:

The amount I had wasn't a lot,
It just seems with age it only takes a little tot.

However, a promise is a promise, so I must rise above my pain,
And produce for you this little refrain.

Now, surely, it must be snuggle-on-the-sofa time.
I do hope you enjoyed this hard-won rhyme.

30

On the day my Dad died, I heard a voice in my ear.
It must have been an angel near.

It said, *Everything will be okay*,
My heart was heavy, but then peace within it lay.

I've not heard any voices since that day.
My husband, though, once heard someone say,

Get off the bus and go and claim your bride.
He did; now he's with me by my side.

Today, within my daily rhyme,
I wanted to take a little time,

To say that there's more to this world than meets the eye.
Angels walk amongst us, and we don't even have to try.

They will turn up when we are most in need.
Now that's a comforting thought indeed.

31

Fiery crimson, or maybe pink rose:
With a touch of colour my confidence grows.

Lips adorned in shades so fine,
Instant glamour and confidence divine.

From ruby reds to pastel pinks,
It's more than makeup; it's how one thinks.

A shade for power; a hue for grace,
It lights up the eyes; transforms the face.

If feeling down, I choose a vibrant hue,
Suddenly the world feels bright and new.

A swipe across lips, the magic begins,
Suddenly, smiles and sassiness within.

In the mirror, I catch a glance,
A hint of lipstick, a daring stance.

Lipstick's joy, it's plain to see,
Transforms the spirit, sets it free.

So wear it proudly, let it show,
The joy of lipstick giving a secret glow.

August

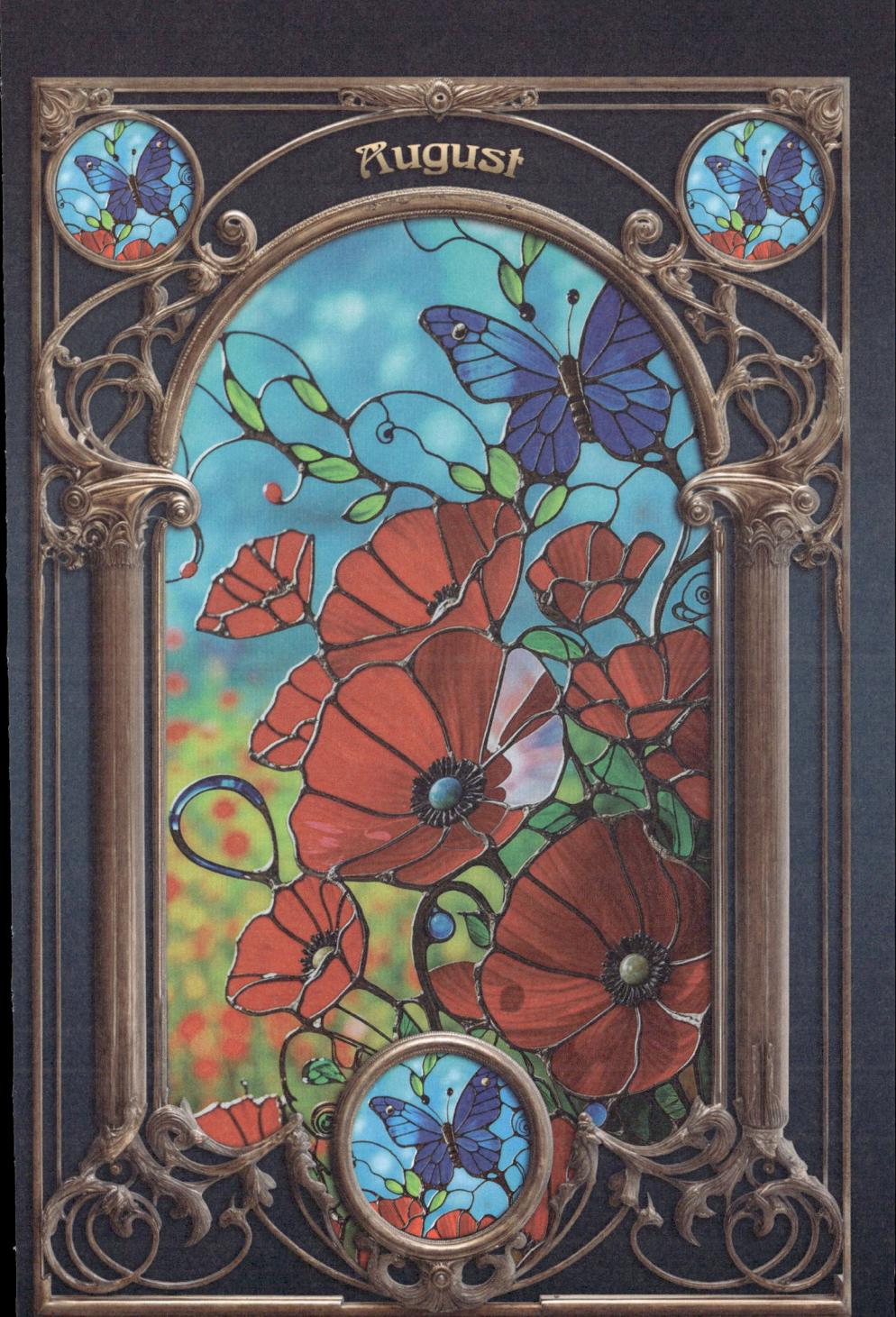

1

Soon I'll move home, and my stuff will go off in a van.
I'll entrust my precious things to a moving man.

Things that I love and see day after day,
Things I'd miss if they went astray.

But it's not expensive objects that have brought me pleasure.
No. If I had to do a review of those things I treasure,

It would be my little pig bought from a charity shop,
Or the plate with a robin on it—Mr. Moving Man, please don't drop!

This, or the mug bought for me by a friend,
Symbolizing a bond that will not end.

At the end of the day, though, as I settle into my new place,
There's one essential I need: my husband's gorgeous face.

2

I got up today feeling poorly and a little blue,
So I decided that 'just enough' would have to do.

Just enough to keep food on the table—
Egg and chips for tea; to produce *Cordon bleu*, I'm not able.

Just enough to provide a little love for my friend—
A quick *I'm here* that's all the support I can extend.

Just enough to keep the wolf from the door—
A brief budget check; I can do no more.

Just enough to keep my rhyming vow,
So thank you for your understanding, and it's bye for now.

3

On National Sunflower Day, let's celebrate a flower full of cheer,
Golden blooms that don't wait for the sun to appear.

They turn to face the light, throughout the day
A symbol of hope and optimism, come what may.

Resilient and strong, through storms they stand,
A beacon of brightness across the land.

They give to butterflies and bees, a nectar sweet,
A giving flower, nature's treat.

Each sunflower is special, made of thousands more,
Ray florets combine, creating something we adore.

Sometimes in life, to truly shine,
We need to be part of something bigger, like this floral design.

So let's honour the sunflower, in fields so bright,
A symbol of tenacity, turning darkness into light.

On this day of celebration, let's remember their way,
And spread hope and joy on National Sunflower Day.

4

In the sky tonight, the new moon's rise,
Is a time for fresh starts, beneath starry skies.

We plant our seeds, with hopes that they'll grow,
Setting clear intentions, letting dreams flow.

Goals in our hearts and projects in view,
We acknowledge our growth and make plans anew.

Since the last new moon, we've blossomed so well,
Now's the time to cast a new spell.

In the quiet, the darkness, where silence has reign,
We rest, recuperate and release all strain.

Meditate deeply, let tension unwind,
In nature's embrace, peace you will find.

Long walks or stillness: surrender with grace,
Take a warm bath, let calmness take place.

A face mask, a massage, a healing retreat,
This is the time to embrace self care, so sweet.

For in this stillness, our powers will grow,
Aided by the new moon's glow.

5

At the Olympics for Team GB, it's been a very good year;
We've all had cause to celebrate and cheer.

Athletes who have achieved their personal best—
It got me thinking, though, about all the rest,

Of the folks in this country who face the day,
With a challenge just as hard in its own way.

The carer who has to carry on,
Even when all hope is gone;

Those so lonely, trying to make a friend,
Hoping for kindness, their isolation to end;

Those queuing at a food bank to feed their kin,
Feeling ashamed, like poverty's a sin.

What our Olympians have had is a helping hand—
Now let's give one to those whose lives ain't so grand.

For all that they are and all that they do,
They deserve a Gold from me and you.

6

When I logged on to X this morning, I had a nice surprise:
Something to put a spring in my step and light in my eyes.

For one of my rhymes had received a like,
From a lovely tweeter called Mike.

Now, this may not seem like a big deal,
But often, when rhyming, I can feel,

A little self-doubt—does anyone take the time,
To read and appreciate my rhyme?

The only way that I can tell if they do,
Is if they press the like button; then I have a positive view,

Of my daily rhyming task.
And though a little like does not seem much to ask,

To me, it means that my writing is not in vain,
And it ensures my resolve doesn't wane.

So today, can you think of one little thing,
That might perhaps make someone's heart sing?

For in this world of noise and clatter,
The small things can truly matter.

7

In the hustle and bustle, we should give a thought,
To the wisdom of sages, their message well taught.

From Socrates' words to Buddha's retreat,
Simplifying life makes our joy more complete.

With fewer possessions, we lighten our load,
Clearing our minds from the chaos they sowed.

Diogenes lived in a barrel so small,
Proving we don't need much to have it all.

Gandhi walked lightly, so humble in dress,
His words of peace can still bless.

Less clutter, more space to breathe and be still,
We find inner peace, and time we can fill.

With moments of nothing, no pressure to do,
Creativity blossoms, old dreams become new.

In silence, we hear our heart's true desire,
A simpler life sets our soul on fire.

So clear out the excess, embrace what is true,
Life's sweetest pleasures will then come to you.

For in the less, we often find more,
A simpler life opens freedom's door.

8

My husband, renovating our house, came across a wall that needed repair.
He had to strip it back to the brick to know what's there,

So that he wasn't leaving it full of holes.
Sometimes we need to do this with our souls.

We need to lay them bare to see what is ours,
Or what dirt we've accumulated that disempowers.

We may be covered in other people's thoughts or deeds,
Stopping us from reaching our potential, meaning our heart bleeds.

When I was younger, I had to seek out therapy,
To wash away the filth and become fully me.

It meant that I could fill my holes and start anew,
So if you face this challenge, good luck to you.

Just remember, as you strip back, whatever you find,
Open your heart to yourself and be kind, kind, kind.

9

On this day of August nine,
A star was born, her voice divine.

Whitney Houston, we remember you,
With songs that made our spirits renew.

From *I Will Always Love You*, so pure and true,
To *Greatest Love of All*, if only you had loved you.

I Wanna Dance with Somebody, a song we loved so,
And you asked the question for us, *How Will I Know*.

You showed us that *All at Once* hearts can heal,
Saving All My Love spoke of how love struck we can feel.

Whitney, your *One Moment in Time* still shines,
A legacy of love, crossing all lines.

Whitney's magic, pure and true,
We salute her spirit too.

Though you're gone, your music remains,
In every note, your spirit sustains.

So on this day, we celebrate your birth,
For you gave us songs of endless worth.

10

Today, I met an angel, disguised as a tradesman.
His name was Gareth, and he turned up in a van.

My internet hub had gone wrong; I had no clue what to do.
It kept mocking me with its orange light, which should be flashing blue.

The minute Gareth arrived, smiling at my door,
I knew that from him, I could expect more.

He clearly was no jobsworth but took pride in his work.
Though it was Friday, he took his time—no way would this man shirk.

Internet fixed in a flash, but it didn't end there;
He took the time to tutor me, showing extra care.

So thank you, Gareth, my angel. To you, your act seemed small,
But to me, you were Heaven-sent to answer my call.

11

Lately, crowds have gathered, filling us all with dread,
But *One bright star is better than a thousand dull moons*, a wise man once said.

This means that in life, we all have a choice:
To stand tall and use our voice,

To support, not denigrate,
It's up to us to make our country great.

So even if our beliefs are considered quite absurd,
Be brave, speak your truth, and ensure your views are heard.

Not by throwing stones or using violence,
But gently, firmly, and giving peace a chance.

Quote by: Matshona Dhliwayo

12

In fields where dreams are spun and skies are blue,
Wildflowers dance, and so can you.

Unbound by rules, you take your stand,
A free spirit flourishing on untamed land.

You, too, can grow wild and reclaim your power,
A spirit unchained, not forced to cower.

Bravely growing wild and free,
In a world plagued by conformity.

For wildflowers thrive where others dare not tread,
In vibrant hues, their beauty widespread.

Embrace your nature, let your spirit bloom,
In every corner, chase away the gloom.

13

When life turns strange and skies go grey,
When words can't chase the pain away,

A cup of tea, you will find,
Is offered up—a gesture kind.

When joy or sorrow knocks on your door,
That simple brew means so much more.

That humble brew is brought with care,
A pause to show that someone's there.

A way to say, *I see your strife*,
A gentle break in rushing life.

Though tea's not my favourite, and I might decline,
Coffee will do to show intentions fine.

For in that cup, what I receive,
Is kindness, love and a space to grieve.

So when the world changes and you're feeling adrift,
That cup of tea is a simple, heartfelt, gift.

14

In the garden, they scurry, they crawl, and they creep,
Tiny invaders, in lines, so deep.

We see them as pests, a nuisance, a bother,
Yet their wisdom and ways we rarely discover.

Oh, the ant, so small yet so grand,
With lessons to teach, if we understand.

With patience in mind, they prepare and plan,
For ants it's never can't, but always can.

Commitment to purpose, they never stray,
Working together, they forge their way.

In teamwork, they thrive, each playing a part,
A model of unity; an undivided heart.

Leadership with humility, the queen leads with grace,
Yet, every ant knows its role and place.

So, while we may see them as pests and just a bother,
These tiny creatures have lessons to offer.

From their world, there's much we could borrow,
For a better today and a brighter tomorrow.

15
We all need a cheerleader in our life,
In times of triumph, or times of strife.

Someone to root for us when things go wrong,
To help us sing our own unique song.

To *Whoop Whoop* us when we have a good day,
Or keep us going when things go astray.

Some folks are lucky; they have one or two,
But here's a secret: your greatest cheerleader can be you.

So however your game of life is going,
Remember to keep that self-love flowing.

Then, whatever the score at the end,
You can still rejoice in you: your own best friend.

16
I don't like to hug; I hope you don't find that shocking.
For those who love to hug, I'm certainly not knocking.

We all have different communication styles, you see,
And having hugs just ain't for me.

I've read all about the health benefits of a hug for body and mind,
But I still don't want them—that doesn't make me cold or unkind.

Those who know me will tell you I'm a good egg through and through;
Not wanting a hug doesn't mean I'm indifferent to you.

My caring style is more through listening and having a chat.
If you want to appreciate me, open your ears and hear me talk about this or that.

There are people in my life that I do give a hug to,
But that's because I love them, and it's not an unpleasant thing to do.

Verbal communication, though, is more my way,
So please consider this rhyme your virtual hug for today.

17

My body's just a vessel—a home for the soul,
A fragile abode where I try to stay whole.

It's been letting me down, I must admit,
With viruses, sprains, and aches that won't quit.

But the soul, oh, the soul, it's a boundless sea,
An infinite source of pure bliss and glee.

The body may suffer, twist, and fall,
But the spirit within stands tall through it all.

For the body's in action, it bears all the strain,
While the soul watches on, untouched by pain.

I'll stay cheerful, despite the aches I endure,
For my spirit is strong, steady, and pure.

So let the body falter, I'll rise above,
With the strength of my soul and a heart full of love.

Though my body is weak, my spirit will sing,
For within me lies an eternal spring.

18

I bought myself a pair of new slippers today; they are very Hollywood.
They are black and fluffy and just make me feel good.

It's funny how the smallest things can affect how we feel,
Like a new lipstick, or getting a great deal.

Even something small can lift my day,
So I hope I remember to appreciate my blessings along the way.

'Cause even when life is hard and our prospects don't look great,
We can always find something to appreciate.

And if we do, with bad times we'll cope,
For when we notice the gifts of life, we're given the greatest gift of hope.

19

Oh, the humble potato, what a treasure to find,
A marvel in the kitchen, versatile with possibilities of every kind.

Mash it up soft, so creamy and light,
Or bake it whole for a comforting bite.

Slice it thin or cut in strips,
Fry it up, and you've got crisps or chips.

Hash browns in the morning, a breakfast delight,
Or, go posh with Dauphinoise with layers just right.

From humble spuds, a spirit takes flight,
Distilled into vodka, pure and bright.

Don't forget, it's also nutritious,
Cheap and abundant—simply delicious.

If you had to survive, it's a definite winner,
For months you could make dinner after dinner.

So here's to the potato, so beloved by me and you,
A kitchen hero through and through!

20

I love autumn when the leaves turn a golden hue,
The air is crisp, the skies are blue,

These past few days have felt so autumny,
Bringing a peace and calm to me.

When summer's warmth has come and gone,
Its fleeting days, I don't dwell on,

For autumn's light, both soft and bright,
Fills my heart with pure delight.

The gentle breeze, the amber hue,
A perfect time for something new.

In autumn's light, I find my way,
And hope for many a golden day.

And as the days grow soft and cool,
I walk with hope, my spirit full.

21

Got up today, spilled my orange juice, laptop not working—life didn't seem a hoot.
Ah! it's going to be one of those days, I thought, but I decided to reboot.

I sat down for a minute or two, took a deep breath in and out,
And thought of all the things in life I have to be glad about.

I allowed myself self-pity, just for a little while,
But then I tried to think of others enduring a greater trial.

I contemplated that somewhere in the world was someone who had no laptop,
No orange juice to greet the day, just a failing crop.

Yes, I realised I was lucky to have these first-world problems in my life.
My day did contain more rubbish, but I'd changed my attitude toward the strife.

When things go wrong, I'll still treat myself with care,
And remember those whose troubles are harder to bear.

22

The one who found my purse in the street when it had gone astray,
The one who found me a parking space for my van on moving day,

The one who finally listened to my internet woes on the phone,
The one who held my hand during an op, so I didn't feel alone,

The one who cheered me up, telling me I looked good,
The one who encouraged me to go on when I didn't think I could,

The one who saved my life in therapy,
The ones—my friends and husband—who give so much to me.

Yes, on National Be an Angel Day, I give thanks to these and more,
For it seems throughout my life, so many have arrived at my door,

Helping me realize that many Angels don't have wings;
They come in many guises and give us many things.

Perhaps today, as I navigate this journey of life,
I can be someone's Angel, give them joy and ease their strife.

23

Happy Birthday, Virgos, it's your special day.
You're practical and kind, in such a thoughtful way.

You're meticulous and wise, with a heart so true,
Loyal and dependable in all that you do.

With your mind so sharp, you always see,
A way to solve every problem, an excellent leader you will always be.

Though sometimes you worry, and can be a bit too neat,
Your caring nature makes you so sweet.

You share this day with stars that shine so bright,
Idris Elba's charm and Shania Twain's delight.

So here's to you, Virgos, on your special day,
May your year be filled with joy in every way!

24

I marched out today with my list of things to do.
I wanted no delays, no waiting in a queue.

I certainly didn't want to stop and chat,
To anyone about this and that.

But the universe had its own plan.
My determination went down the pan.

You see, I met so many folk I know along the way;
I had to take a different attitude to my day.

To ignore these pals would have been rude;
I had to breathe and take an interlude,

And put my list to one side and adopt a different intent:
To value the folks in my town who are Heaven-sent.

So I chilled and followed my heart instead of my mind,
Lingered a while and engaged in chat, positive and kind.

The magic of this, a lesson bound to please:
When I went back to the list, I completed it with ease.

25

In the garden, small they grow,
Herbs with secrets, powers to show.

Tiny leaves with mighty might,
In the kitchen and in health, they shine bright.

Rosemary, tall, with scent so sweet,
In roasts and breads, it can't be beat.

But don't forget, in days of old,
It eased the mind, or so we're told.

Lavender, fragrant, soft and sweet,
Soothes the soul, brings restful sleep.

In desserts, it adds a flair,
But it's more than scent—it cleanses the air.

Dandelion, called a weed by name,
Yet in a tea, it finds its fame.

A liver's friend, and skin so clear,
This humble plant is one to cheer.

A sprig of thyme, so humble, slight,
Can season soups, make fevers right.

Basil, green with spicy taste,
In pasta grand, a feast embraced.

Yet in its leaves, a tonic there,
To lift the mood when hearts are filled with care.

Mint, the cool and soothing touch,
In summer drinks, we love so much.

But in the chest, when breath is tight,
It brings relief; the air made light.

So with herbs as with people, look within,
For value hides beneath the skin.

26

Every day when I rise,
I put a sparkle in my eyes.

By doing the thing that brings me joy,
A pleasure that no care can destroy.

I dance. This connects me with my soul,
Takes all the pieces of me and makes them whole.

It makes me feel young, though that's not the case;
When dancing, I think that life I can ace.

On days when I'm poorly and can't have a twirl,
I'm definitely a different kind of girl.

I feel blue and kinda flat,
Find it hard to deal with this and that.

If I dance, though, I can touch the sky,
So I'll keep dancing until I die.

(and then hopefully in Heaven, too!)

27

Hello friend! Please take the time,
To join me in a daily rhyme,

To uplift and maybe make you look,
To find the gold amongst the muck.

I take a quirky view of life you'll find.
Always positive, always kind.

Now join me so we can explore,
Simple things which offer more.

28

In gardens far and wide across the land,
Each seed is sown with a tender hand.

Then we wait, we water, we tend the earth,
Believing each living thing has its worth.

But still, the truth is hard to know:
Why some things bloom, and others go.

In warmth, in light, in fertile ground—
Some never rise, some don't rebound.

So it is with our friends and kin:
We try our best to help them win.

We feed them hope, we light their way,
We shield them from the harshest day.

But choice and chance, and winds unknown,
May shape them far from what we've sown.

We give them the tools, our time, and grace,
But not every soul finds its flowering place.

So in the end, we must release,
And hope our care will yield some peace.

For control is a myth, a gardener's dream—
We can only foster, not force their gleam.

And so I share, with quiet sigh,
Some lavender I planted has died.

Right next to one that's strong, alive—
Both side by side, yet just one would thrive.

It's nature's way, a garden's song:
Some truths remain a mystery all along.

29

Nelson Mandela wrote, *Don't Play Small*.
That doesn't mean rising above them all.

It means being beautifully, uniquely you,
And honouring your gifts, whatever you do.

In this world, you have a special place,
Something at which you simply ace.

So whether it's line dancing or making wine,
Give the world your gifts and shine, Shine, SHINE!

30

Today I met a girl called Roxy on a train,
We probably won't meet again.

But for half an hour we talked and shared,
And we both engaged; showed we cared.

We bonded over our lipstick choice,
To our trivia and deep we gave voice.

Though a brief encounter it made me think,
Strangers can move you, even if they're gone in a blink.

31

Some strive to make the world a better place,
They go green or a statue they deface.

Some in foreign climes do toil,
Some protest and shout, *Just stop oil!*

These humans are trying as humans should.
What will their legacy be, will it be good?

I want mine to be, when folks bring me to mind,
Nothing grand, just a statement, *Oh, she was kind.*

September

1
What ya doing this weekend?,
Asks a colleague or a friend.

They tell you of a fabulous invite,
Or some event that should excite.

You feel as if your weekend is just so-so,
You've got a bad case of FOMO.

But wait, there's another point to see:
You're the winner, no show, no act, you just get to BE!

2
Didn't want to get up today, things felt bleak,
But someone had to do the shopping for the week.

So off I went to tackle the aisle,
Who'd have thought that there I'd find a smile?

But over the intercom came tune after banging tune,
I gave a little wiggle, started feeling over the moon.

So if you find that somehow your life ain't smooth,
Head for that aisle, dance with your trolley, get into your groove.

3
Sundays fill some people with dread,
If that's you, get into your heart and out of your head.

Stop filling your world with woe,
And think on the things that you love so.

All the things that today have been Heaven-sent,
Instead of rehearsing a Monday lament.

So, instead of wasting your precious hours,
Don't let your day be another thing that the system devours.

Limit yourself to a 10-minute moan,
Then walk, laugh, hug, and kiss; claim this Sunday as your own.

4

I saw a list the other day,
Of things people wish were on their way.

To make their dreams come true,
Like cars and houses and fancy things to do.

I must admit it made me think,
Somewhere in the world, someone's wishing for water to drink,

Wholesome food and a home without war.
So I'm taking the time to think what I'm grateful for,

'Cause I'm blessed right now in a million ways.
I'll remember this if ever, with longing, into the future, I gaze.

5

Creativity should be a pleasure,
Something to cherish and to treasure.

So don't make what you're doing such a chore,
As that will dishearten you and bore.

So find something you love to do,
Something that comes from the heart of you,

And then dive right in and go with the flow,
Express yourself, 'cause only you know what you know.

6

I'm a water sign, and it's been dry—
No clouds, no tears to cleanse the sky.

The Earth is parched, my heart the same—
We both are aching for the rain.

She thirsts for drops to cleanse her skin—
Like I do, when I hold tears in.

When I can't cry, my spirit dries,
A storm withheld behind my eyes.

But tears, like rain, can clear the haze,
And soften hearts in tender ways.

Rain feeds the roots, and tears heal too;
They clear the air, let us start anew.

When feelings flood, we start to grow—
Let the rain, and my tears, freely flow.

Don't hold back your tears; embrace the pain.
And like a garden, you'll bloom again.

7

Sometimes as we walk along the street,
A passing stranger, we may meet.

And if we're feeling chipper, we might smile,
Making them feel seen and worthwhile.

Yes, smiling can often feel quite brave,
But do it today; for someone's life, it might save.

For in their mind, you might plant a seed
Of friendship and hope, something surely that we all need.

8

A friend of mine, who owns a great clothes shop,
Told me there's something she wants to see stop:

She serves lovely women, all shapes and sizes—
Boho, chic, young & old, they come in all guises.

But no matter how beautiful they are,
They exhibit behaviour so bizarre:

However great they look, they are not content.
Come on, girls, walk tall, for you, my Angels, were Heaven-sent!

9

I dance every day to bring me joy,
And put a spring in my step, no care can destroy.

It's not to stay slim or to exercise,
But to keep that sparkle in my eyes.

As I dance, sometimes tame, sometimes wild,
I get back in touch with my inner child.

Yes, dancing makes my heart and soul sing,
And rings my bell... Ding-a-ling-ling!

10

I recently got a test on my DNA,
Hoping to find exotic ancestry along the way.

And the result that was the most striking,
It turns out that in fact I'm part Viking.

But I've not started wearing fur or playing a horn,
'Cause I believe that no matter where I was born,

There's more than my bloodline that makes me, me.
There's a million little quirks, like my love for Afternoon tea.

So if your search for meaning leads you to your past,
Try looking closer to home, for it's YOUR gifts to this world that will last.

11

Have you got the Monday blues?
Wishing you were in someone else's shoes?

Did you find it hard to get out of bed?
Are you dreading the week ahead?

I've got for you a little strategy:
Rename Monday *MOONday*, because that's what it used to be.

The moon is cheering, magical, and bright,
Dwell on this wonder in the world, and your Monday may turn out alright.

12

And you thought that Tuesdays were not special at all,
That they're like Cinderella before she went to the ball.

Well, please allow me to set you right.
Here are some facts to make this Tuesday seem bright.

Today is the National Day of Encouragement.
When someone's feeling low, we can let them know they were Heaven-sent.

It's also National Chocolate Milkshake Day.
Now, a milkshake to me says fun and play.

So see this Tuesday's got a lot to recommend.
Though don't get too excited, it's also National Gym day, my friend!

So if you or another are feeling low,
Get encouraged, have a chocolate shake, then off to the gym you go!

13
We get so stressed out in these lives we live;
Sometimes, a little thing seems hard to forgive.

But try to be nice to those you meet along the way;
You don't know what they're dealing with in their day.

They may have received some bad news,
Or be struggling to buy their kids new shoes.

Buddha taught kind acts count no matter how small,
And if you feel low, practising kindness can make you feel 10 feet tall.

So whatever struggles you have on your mind,
Take care of you, then to others be kind.

14
If you're feeling out of sorts and don't know what to do,
Seek out the words of that well-known sage, Mr. Winnie-the-Pooh.

'Cause it turns out that, in fact, Pooh was a very wise bear,
And he could truly help you with every tricky care.

For every little thing he said,
Could help you clear your very muddled head.

He pointed out, *Always remember you are braver and smarter than you think*,
So get your Pooh book out and, from his font of wisdom, have a lovely drink.

15

Happy Friday! How's your weekend looking?
Have you got an exciting restaurant booking?

Or is the weekend stretching ahead,
With nothing beckoning but sofa and bed?

Kahlil Gibran wrote, *The heart is refreshed by the little things*,
For me, there's nothing better than pink sprinkled doughnut rings.

Having one of those will get my weekend off to a great start.
What is it that would lift your spirits and refresh your heart?

Is it brightly painting your toes,
Or checking how your garden grows?

A glass of wine or a cheeky beer,
Try a little thing to celebrate: the weekend's here!

16

My friend sent me a pic today,
Of a Grecian paradise-her holiday stay.

I'm sat here in a rainy town.
Who could blame me for feeling down?

There is, though, another way to look at this:
Soon my love will wake; and I'll give him a kiss.

We'll snuggle on the sofa, we won't stray far,
'Cause paradise can be found right where you are.

17
You want to dance and get it right,
But the fear of judgment invokes such fright.

The key is to treat the task as fun,
Then your own approval you'll have won.

Nobody is looking over your shoulder,
Remembering this; it will make you bolder.

So put on that music and flex that knee,
Shout, *The only person I wanna please is me.*

18
If Monday feels drab and bleak as can be,
Then try a little colour therapy.

Red will get you out of bed;
And get you moving when you want to stay snuggled instead.

Wear red to feel young, invigorated, bold,
And able to tell truths that need to be told.

Wear red today; give your week a kickstart;
You'll attract, turn heads, but don't go breaking a heart.

19
Summer was short, and autumn has started.
Now winter approaches, but don't be downhearted.

Though it's easy to succumb to the gloom,
For autumn's splendour, let's make some room.

Before trees are bare and first frosts appear,
Appreciate the autumnal gifts that bring us cheer:

Berries, golden leaves, and a crackling bonfire,
And all the hot chocolate our hearts desire-with marshmallows, of course!

Wearing our favourite jumpers, spiders' webs on the wall.
If we dwell on these then for autumn we will Fall!

20
Happy Wednesday—a day full of hope,
That maybe for two more days you can cope.

A day that lifts the spirits and seems to say,
Keep going, Brave Heart, for the weekend's on its way.

So how's your week been going so far?
Whether stressful, mundane, or bizarre,

I wish you well for the next 48 hours,
Then you can stop and smell the flowers.

21
Some days in life can seem quite hard,
There's a problem with your credit card.

So to the bank, you try to get through,
But there's only a machine to talk to you.

You just need a human to be kind,
And listen to what's on your mind.

Frustrated on the phone, you can help your stress stop,
Take a deep breath in, smile, and let your shoulders drop.

Remember the quote, *Don't let the Bs grind you down*,
You're worth more than this, get polishing that invisible crown.

22
Not all angels have wings,
They look like ordinary folk doing ordinary things.

Like the colleague who tells you *Go get a drink*,
When on a tough day you feel on the brink.

Or the lady who lets you go in front in the queue,
On the day you have a million things to do.

Think of the guy who gave you a seat on the train,
'Cause he somehow noticed that you were in pain.

These are little things that mean so much more.
Today, who could you be an angel for?

23
It's the autumn equinox—a day of balance,
From tomorrow, the night will advance.

And as birds start to migrate,
We begin to hibernate.

With candles lit, we cosy-in,
Determined that the dark won't win.

The autumn equinox, a reminder to pause and hear,
The whispers of the Earth, and the shifting of the year.

24
The Bangles sang, *I wish it was Sunday*,
Implying it's a day for fun and play.

Sometimes, though, Sundays just get lost.
Amidst a sea of to-dos, but at what cost?

We start our week exhausted from the start,
That's no good for our head or heart.

So today, unfurl that furrowed brow.
Relax, recharge, and be here now.

25
Today is One-Hit Wonder Day,
When we celebrate the stars who brought us joy along the way.

They knocked it out of the park just one time,
And some of those songs are truly sublime.

Opening my eyes and making me see,
that I've been to paradise, but *I've Never Neen to Me*.

Though flashes in the pan, they helped us feel high,
And to this day they lift us like the *Spirit in the Sky*.

So, download, or listen on CD, vinyl or tape,
With a One-Hit Wonder, the Monday blues you'll *Escape*.

26
Are you going shopping today? Then open your eyes,
To something other than those bargain buys.

Seeing a lady in a rainbow outfit so bright,
Reminds you that to others you can be a source of light.

Meeting a friend for coffee and a chat:
A simple thing can make us happy—you can learn that.

If, on a whim, you buy something to bring your partner pleasure,
You can create a moment that you'll both treasure.

It doesn't matter if you return home empty-handed:
Your point of view will have expanded.

27

As winter approaches and the sky turns grey,
You may be packing your summer clothes away.

But before you get out the black, give it some thought,
'Cause there's an important message Colour Therapy has taught.

And that is, what you wear affects your mood:
Dull colours can bring you down and make you brood.

So maybe keep out that yellow top,
don a bright pink scarf, and the winter blues you will stop.

28

Happy Birthday to you if it's yours today.
You're a Libra, known for their love of fair play,

And wanting to bring balance to every situation,
You're one of the most popular star signs in the nation.

You have emotional intelligence which makes you caring,
And your creative flair can make you daring.

Gandhi and John Lennon shared your sign:
Obviously you've got a sense of the divine.

Interested in rising from the quagmire and looking above,
You truly embody the tenet, *All You Need is Love*.

29

Today is a full harvest super moon, a sight to behold,
And maybe its light will help us feel bold,

Enough to contemplate what we've done, for we know,
That it's true: we usually reap what we sow.

The moon can leave us emotionally reeling,
And highlight each and every feeling,

So as you head out for your Friday night fun,
Take care, have no regrets, when you're greeted by tomorrow's sun.

30

Saturday's a day to savour and play,
With sunshine and joy, come what may.

But what if yours is just a list of to-dos?
For, sometimes, we need to do things we don't choose.

If that's the case, then carve out some time,
For yourself, 'cause taking care of you ain't a crime.

Even just sitting down with a lovely brew,
Will help you unwind and your spirit renew.

Make sure a little pleasure for yourself you are seizing,
Then your Saturday will flow and be more pleasing.

October

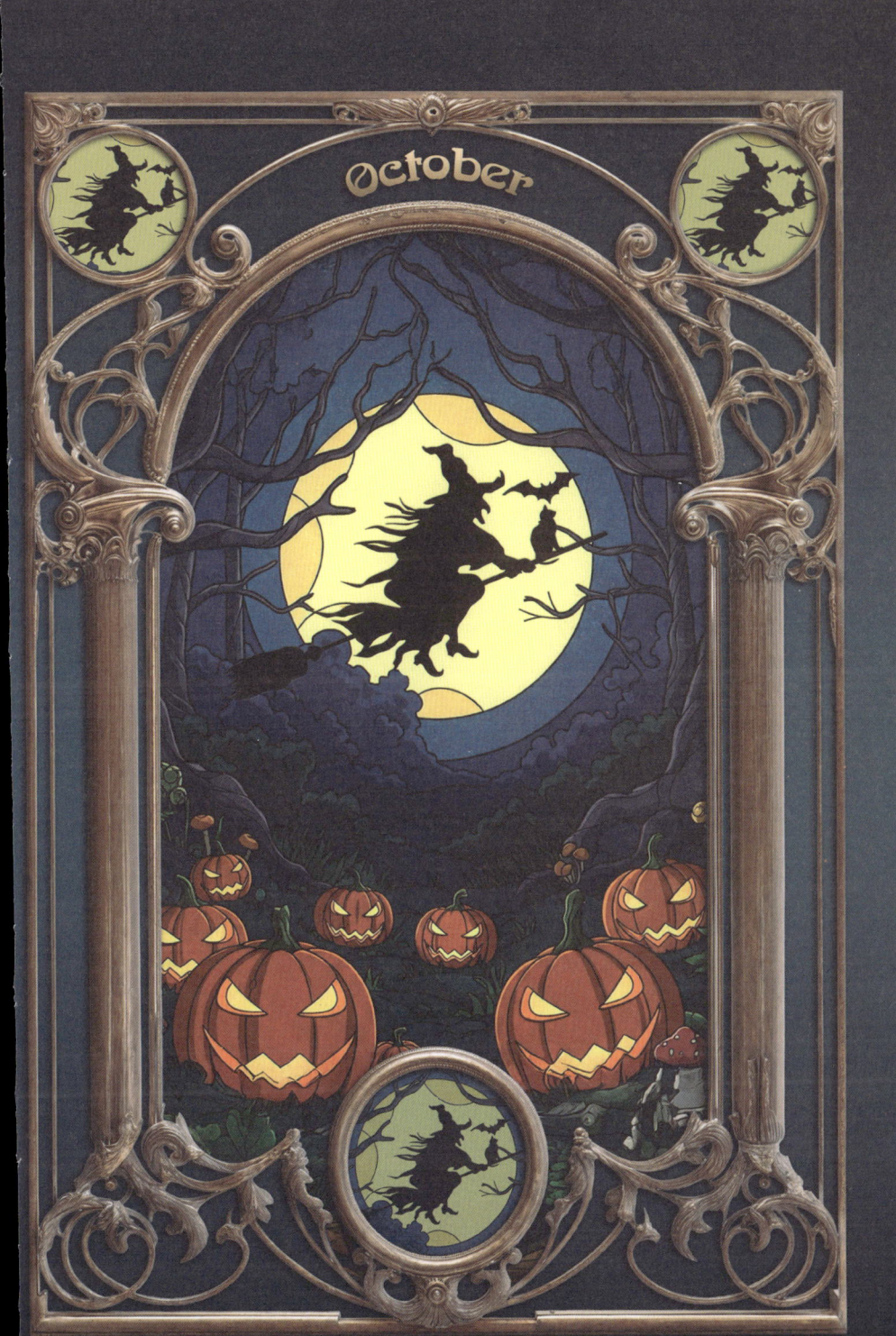

1

Last night, I watched Strictly, and on the show,
Some rabbits in headlamps; some in the flow.

Dance like nobody's watching, so the saying goes,
But what if you're shaking from head to toes?

We can all hold back, fearing others' judgment,
But here's some advice that is kindly meant,

If you've got a challenge to face,
Do this one thing, and you will ace:

Remember in life when you got a *10*,
Feel it, relive it, and you'll do it with Zen.

2

Happy Monday! Was your weekend all you'd hoped for,
Or did it leave you disappointed, wanting more?

Here's a thought to give your heart a lift:
The present is called the present because it's a gift.

So, don't dwell on what could have been,
Or fear the future, as yet unseen;

Cherish your Monday; look for the good in all that you do,
Then with a smile on your face you'll make it through.

3
October is a month for storms and rain;
The weather sure can be a pain.

Let's remember what the great Dolly Parton said:
There ain't no rainbows without rain, a thought to keep in our head.

If you're sad that summer's finally gone,
And you have to put the heating on,

Look closely and see there are wonders to behold,
And things to warm your heart against the cold:

Starlings murmurating, berries on the trees,
And crisp moonlit nights—sights that never fail to please.

4
This is no ordinary Wednesday: it's World Animal Day,
Marked on the feast day of St. Francis, who tried to show us the way,

To kindness for all creatures with whom this planet we share,
And there's a lot we can do to show that we care.

I don't mean watching *Babe* or *Chicken Run*,
Though both films are truly great fun;

Sign a petition to free chickens from cages;
Speak up against animal cruelty that enrages.

Go veggie; you will find meals that are yum;
Visit a shelter and make an unloved pet your chum.

Don't buy creams tested on animals to slap on your face;
Just for one day, in your heart, give animals a special place.

5

When you see a Butterfly, pause and think what it's been through.
Though it looks so beautiful, every c to me and you,

It never started out that way:
Once a caterpillar, we wouldn't have given it the time of day.

Then in its cocoon it turned itself to mush,
And emerged looking beautiful, radiant and lush.

So be kind to yourself whatever stage you're at,
Today a caterpillar—tomorrow a Butterfly, that's a fact.

6

Today, I watched *The Wizard of Oz*, a cinematic delight,
It prompted me to wonder which character feels just right.

Not the Wicked Witch, that's quite clear,
I'd prefer to be the Wizard, spreading joy and cheer.

Though sometimes fear creeps in, like the Cowardly Lion,
I strive to be courageous, with nerves made of iron.

With empathy and kindness, a heart I possess,
Not the Tin Man's emptiness; nor the Scarecrow's need to impress.

But like the Scarecrow, I yearn for knowledge, it's true,
I guess if I were to choose, I'd be a mix of all, wouldn't you?

Deep down inside and wherever we roam,
We're all like Dorothy, finding *There's No Place Like Home*.

7

Outside of our window, we have a lovely view,
A little lavender plant, fragrant and blue.

Bees love it, and butterflies too.
If you get a burn, it can heal you.

If stressed, its oil can help you chill.
When in need of soothing, lavender fits the bill.

Having trouble drifting off to sleep?
Lavender's better than counting sheep.

Yes, lavender from nature truly is a gift.
Plant some and give your mind, body, and soul a lift.

8

Last night on Strictly, some stood proud and tall,
Others, sadly, took a fall.

One thing is sure: the applause was resounding,
Though all their feet took a pounding,

And may need some tender caring,
Though to fiddle with feet does take daring.

So it's fitting to remember on National Podiatry Day,
Those who administer in a kindly way,

To folks in need of TLC for their feet,
So they can keep dancing to that funky beat!

9

George Eliot wrote, *It's never too late to become the person you always thought you could be*,
Sorry, George, I don't agree.

For even if we nurture a dream in our heart,
Whether we fulfil it, or not, is determined by where we start.

Try telling the boy hunting on the African plain,
That it's easy to be a doctor; that he can start again.

To say it's all about positive thinking and *just believe*,
Is crass, unthinking, and very naive.

Nonetheless, it's important that we strive,
To keep some part of our dream alive.

So, I may never dance in the Bolshoi Ballet,
But I think I'll sign up for a tap dancing class today.

Because however small a step we take,
A big difference to our souls it will make.

10

Winston Churchill wrote, *If you're going through Hell, keep going*,
But what if your energy and strength ain't flowing?

Help is the hardest word to say, that's true.
Be brave and say it; there's someone there for you.

The world is full of people whose hearts are kind,
They will listen to what's on your mind.

Be it a stranger or a friend,
Reach out, and your loneliness will end.

For my lovely, you may doubt your worth,
But you're unique, and only you can fill your spot on this Earth!

11

The leaves are turning brown, and the skies are turning grey.
You need some green to brighten your day.

Green is the colour of spring and hope,
With winter's gloom and grey it will help you cope.

Buy a green cushion for your sofa; or a green scarf to wear,
Green's a nurturing colour that will help you care.

For yourself, when you're feeling low,
It's the colour of balance and going with the flow.

The smell of green is peppermint,
Inhale and in your eyes, you'll see a glint.

So as we snuggle in our nests and hibernate,
Liven up your world, with green as your mate.

12

Kahlil Gibran wrote, *In the sweetness of friendship, let there be laughter, and sharing of pleasures.*
And laughing with a friend for me is one of life's greatest treasures.

Turns out, though, that there's more to laughter than meets the eye.
It can help with pain relief and make you go from low to high.

Laughter Therapy is something that you can do,
(You might feel silly, but it's a natural cure for feeling blue).

So tune in to your old favourite comedy on the telly,
And have a giggle, a chuckle, or even a deep laugh from your belly.

13
I love words and their etymology.
Where words come from fascinates me.

For all words, even boring ones, have origins,
Like my favourite word, *Shenanigans*,

It's a word from San Francisco, Spain, or maybe the Emerald Isle.
Whenever I hear it, it makes me smile.

And though I admit I'm no linguist,
Words delight and excite me; you get the gist.

I know lots of words started off Latin or Greek,
So look there first if a word's beginnings you seek.

What's your favourite word? It might not be as fancy as mine.
It may just be *Home*, a simple word, but so divine.

14
When out of sorts, I have found,
Using crystals from the sacred ground,

Helps me open a healing door.
For every ill there's a crystal cure:

Citrine will leave you positive and filled with fun,
And help you to discover your inner sun.

Rose Quartz is good to heal a broken heart,
So in matters of love, you'll make a new start.

Amethyst is like a cooling shower of rain:
Refreshing after stress, and easing pain.

Remember: if a crystal calls to you and says, *Choose me*,
That's the one that you need; buy it; it was meant to be.

15

My friend, Arthur, has two left feet,
And when he dances, he always always misses the beat.

But Arthur doesn't care as he twirls around the floor;
It's something about him I admire and adore.

For which of us has the courage to just let go;
To stop worrying about what others think and go with the flow?

Whether in life or in dancing, let Arthur be our inspiration,
For it's courage, not perfection, that deserves aspiration.

So, as we watch those adventurers aim for the Glitter Ball,
Remember: it's how many times you get up, not how many you fall!

16

Oscar Wilde was born on this day,
He was a master of the quote to show us the way:

Be yourself; everybody else is taken,
Helps us with doubt being overtaken.

We are all in the gutter, but some of us are looking at the stars,
Hopefully true in daily life, not just in bars.

Some cause happiness wherever they go, and some cause happiness whenever they go,
So let us strive to be the former, and seeds of kindness sow.

Finally, *To love oneself is the beginning of a life-long romance*,
So let's heed his words, with self-care and respect in life advance.

17
On my wedding day, I had a poem called *Risk* read out,
For on that day, I risked my heart, no doubt.

And though I will never swing from a bungee rope,
I like to think that with a little fear, I can cope.

'Cause it's scary sometimes to speak what's true,
Like telling a friend they've not been there for you;

Or admitting sometimes that you feel a bit lost,
Maybe standing up for someone, no matter what the cost.

But unless you risk, the reward you may never know,
So take a little risk today: go YOU, go!

By the way, the reward for my risk on that wedding day:
A man who treasures my heart, come what may.

18
Never forget where you've come here from, sang Take That.
But what if where you came from didn't put out a Welcome mat?

On the day that you took your place on this Earth,
What if there were people who made you doubt your worth?

Maybe then you should forget and look ahead;
Create a brighter tomorrow for yourself instead.

Like a warrior, keep fighting—past demons you can tame,
'Cause no matter where you came from, the future's yours to claim.

19

Birds—so infinite in their variety,
Every day bring such joy to me.

The Pied Wagtail with its distinctive wiggle,
Always makes me want to smile and giggle.

And the very small but beautiful Blue Tit,
With me, it is a massive hit.

Then there's the Robin that everyone loves best,
Reminding me of Christmas with its ruddy vest.

Even the humble pigeon has its place,
Looking proud, its visits we should embrace.

Yes, birds can give us so much pleasure,
Let's cherish them and treat them like an earthly treasure.

20

Some folk do jobs that attract admiration,
They are lauded and applauded across the nation.

But here's another point of view:
Your job matters, whatever you do.

If someone did not collect our bin,
A rubbish state we would be in.

And when we go out for a meal,
Our server can influence the way we feel.

A smile from the cashier as we pay,
Can turn around a difficult day.

Whatever you do for a living, give it some heart,
As if you were crafting a work of art.

In the tapestry of life, realise how important you are,
You're an essential thread, like a shining star.

21

How are you today? Feeling in the pink, I hope.
If not, no worries because here's a tip to help you cope,

With feeling drab and downbeat,
Or when stress is making you feel the heat.

The colour pink can get you back on track,
And put love into your world if that's what you lack.

For pink's not just the colour of Barbie;
It's one of the stars of Colour Therapy.

At providing self-care and comfort, it does excel,
And can make you feel flirty and fun as well!

So bring some pink into your world with some lippy or a sock,
Then, like Barbie and Ken, you'll be skipping around the block!

22

All the days of our life are like a dance,
We sometimes move with ease; we sometimes take a chance.

At other times, we falter and fumble.
Life's a manic quick step; we fear a tumble.

Through a lovely day, like a waltz, we glide,
Our feet barely touching and our hearts filled with pride.

And, on occasion, we reveal just who we are:
Unashamed, uninhibited—life's a Cha-Cha-Cha.

Surely, we all long for an American Smooth flow,
Every step we take is faultless, and we're in the know.

But whatever dance your day is, keep this in mind:
Your beat is unique and your dance one of a kind.

23
Monday is so reviled, it needs a rebrand.
So what name could we give it to make it seem grand?

What about *Bun-day*, go treat yourself to your favourite cake,
Or *Fun-day*, watch a film that with laughter makes your belly ache.

Won-day: celebrate a small victory,
Nothing big—maybe just having fish & chips for tea.

And Monday could be *Sunny-day*, if you give it the holiday vibe:
Wear a Hawaiian shirt, and maybe a Mojito imbibe.

If we view Monday in a different way,
It might become our favourite day!

24
Happy Birthday to you today; you're a Scorpio,
One of the bravest and most loyal folks we could know.

As a Scorpio, you don't play games in a relationship;
You're honest and shoot from the hip.

Once you make up your mind to love someone,
You do it with passion, and that love is never gone.

Ambitious and determined, going for your goal,
Easily slighted, you're a very deep soul.

Sharing your birthday with Katy Perry, a *Firework*,
And Gordon Ramsay, who from the truth doesn't shirk.

Enjoy your day, Scorpio, for to entrance you never fail,
And sometimes it's good to have that sting in your tail!

25

Andy Warhol used soup cans as art,
And I think soup's a food of the heart.

For what is better on a winter's day,
Than a bowl of soup to keep the chills away?

The variety of soups means it doesn't bore,
No matter how many you've tried, there's always one more.

Whether it's posh onion soup with a crouton,
Or the more exotic Chinese wonton.

With so many soup flavours to delight,
Why not try a Spicy Parsnip or Creamy veg tonight?

And you will feel a warmth grow within,
Yes, the humble can of soup, not just art, it's soul reviving.

26

Each day I write a rhyme to uplift and amuse,
Today my mind's a blank, deserted by my muse.

There must be a way to get my words to flow,
Something clever used by writers in the know.

Surely, sometimes they all struggle, even famous Will,
I'm sure that there were days he stared blankly at his quill.

Stephen King in his book *On Writing*:
Revealed how to stimulate and make a story frightening.

But, alas, I admit I never read that book,
So I suppose what I'm seeking is a little bit of luck.

But wait, it's a miracle, a rhyme I have produced,
Yes, the muse is back; I'm on fire; my rhyme is fully juiced.

27
It's Friday again—time to forget your workday troubles.
But this Friday, my friend, has added bubbles.

For today is Global Champagne Day,
Time to honour a drink that epitomizes fun and play.

Though made in France, it's a drink beloved by our nation,
For it's a sign of good times, fun and celebration.

And if your week's been a strain on your brain or heart,
Well, heed well the words of Napoleon Bonaparte:

In victory, you deserve Champagne; in defeat, you need it.
Go on, treat yourself—to Champagne's charms, you should submit!

28
Tonight, the clocks turn back: it's that time of year.
Some find things bleak and can't see the cheer.

In darker evenings and shorter days,
If we look hard, though, we will see the ways,

To view this adjustment a gift;
And not succumb to gloom, but our spirits lift.

We've an extra hour to do with as we will,
Maybe take the dog for a walk, or just sit still.

Or call up an old friend and have a chat;
Perhaps take a long, luxurious bath—how about that?

This hour's yours for the taking; don't let it spoil.
If you claim and use it, winter's misery you'll foil.

29

On Strictly last night, there was Halloween fun,
Whilst some stars faltered, some shone like the sun.

The costumes were designed to give us a fright,
But it was the fear of failure that did some dances blight.

And though I don't believe in ghosts or ghouls,
At times, fear can make us all feel like fools.

But as Babe Ruth said, *Don't let the fear of failure hold you back*.
So, let's get back into our groove and get our life dance back on track.

30

Trees, of which I am a fan,
Have suffered so greatly at the hand of man.

First, ancients were felled for HS2;
Then the Sycamore Gap was butchered, out of the blue.

When we lose trees, we lose a part of our soul,
For by loving trees, we become more whole.

Trees breathe out tales of history,
A testament to life's grand mystery.

Let's revere these arboreal souls,
Their wisdom vast; their history rolls.

In their silence, a majestic trace,
They impart resilience, time's steady embrace.

31

Today is Halloween, but it's also National Magic Day,
So if Halloween's too dark for you, maybe there's another way,

To enjoy the magic and mystery of this Earth,
And instead of fear, enjoy the mirth.

Yes, today's a day for a treat or a trick,
So let's choose a trick performed so slick,

By someone whose job it is to bring pleasure,
An amateur or a national treasure.

Watch a trick or two on YouTube tonight,
Have a laugh, have fun; instead of darkness, embrace the light.

November

1

Are you dreading winter? Does it all seem so grey?
Here's a simple remedy: put some orange in your day.

Think of juicy oranges ripening in the Med,
Now, doesn't that put some happy thoughts in your head?

You see, orange is cheerful and rejuvenates your soul.
If you're feeling lost, it'll help you feel more whole.

It's a playful colour that can give you lots of zing,
Helps you be creative if you want to paint or sing.

When winter's chills make you shrink into your skin,
Orange will get you active, give you warmth within.

But what if wearing orange is a move far too bold?
Well, with a candle or crystal, you'll be armed against the cold.

Orange may not make everybody rave,
But in the colder months, your vim and vigour it will save.

2

Karen Carpenter sang that rainy days always got her down.
If another wet autumn makes you want to frown,

I'm going to suggest a strategy: make a list,
Of things you love—you get the gist.

Take some quality time to compile,
A note of all the things that make you smile.

You could go all Julie Andrews and think of your favourite things,
That when done or seen, your heart sings.

Don't neglect little wins, like your morning coffee,
Or a remembered joke to fill your heart with glee.

For with a little effort, we can ward off that pain,
And look for rainbows in the rain.

3

When we're out and about and meet someone new,
One of the first things we ask is, *What do you do?*

And when they tell us, we make an assessment:
Are they worthy of note? We make the judgment.

I'd like to ask you, though, to give this a try:
A little something to alter your view of passers-by.

Next time you meet a stranger, ask them who they ARE,
And you might find you're dealing with a superstar;

Not a B- or C-list celebrity,
But someone who's funny, smart, and as kind as can be.

A survivor, a carer, an everyday hero,
Someone whose acts are more than just for show.

So when we greet each other, let's forget our roles,
Let's get to know each other's hearts, minds, and souls.

4

Have you ever heard someone say as a joke,
Are your chakras in balance?, designed to provoke?

Then let me let you in on a little secret:
Your chakras can help you be the best you yet.

In your body, they are energy centres, seven,
They can keep you grounded or have you reaching for Heaven.

Your throat chakra is blue and governs communication,
Green is at your heart and seeks affirmation.

Yes, you've got a stunning rainbow within,
That, if balanced, in life will help you win.

If you want to know more about this magical thing,
Give an acupuncturist or colour healer a ring.

5

Last night on Strictly, the dancers put on quite a display,
Moves that lit up the night, like the fireworks we'll watch today.

Some spun like a Catherine Wheel,
Their Viennese Waltz enchanted; we were made to feel.

Bravo, the Sparklers, who burned so bright,
In the Samba, with fun, our passion they did ignite.

The Bangers come and go in a flash,
As in the Quickstep, around the floor, they would dash.

Finally, the Rockets, reaching so high for that glitter ball,
For their Charleston moves, we did fall.

Yes, tonight, as crackling fireworks fill the air,
Let's remember the Strictly celebs who dream and dare.

The ones who every Saturday bring joy and light
The living fireworks, a magical sight.

6

It's Monday, and I hope you don't have the Monday Blues.
If you do, here's a revelation: your attitude is yours to choose.

'Cos though your heart may have sunk hearing that alarm ring,
Monday still holds the promise to make your heart sing.

It's an opportunity with hope to look ahead,
Instead of the same old, same old, we might dread.

Plan for the week, make a review,
Of things that you can look forward to.

And if there's nothing positive you can find,
Then resolve to spend the week to yourself being kind.

Seize this day to seize the week; let your dreams soar,
Monday can be the kick-off to so much more.

7

Shakespeare is often known as the nation's favourite bard,
Though many avoid him because they find his works too hard.

In fact, many sayings which we use today,
Originated in a Shakespeare play.

Yes, he wrote of a *Heart of Gold* and *For goodness sake*,
And the wisdom of *All's well that ends well*, a point we all could take.

If when someone mentions Shakespeare, you say *It's Greek to me*,
The irony is that he gave you the words to express this plea.

Finally, he coined the notion that *Brevity is the soul of wit*.
So, here endeth today's rhyme—yes, that's it!

8

If you're in a quandary and don't know what to do,
Might I suggest you try a little blue?

Blue is the colour of wisdom and thought;
It can help relax your muscles when they're feeling taut.

It's a colour so peaceful and calming,
Helping you speak your truth, coming off as charming.

So if your world's so stressful it makes you want to cry,
Close your eyes, breathe, and contemplate a cloudless, blue, blue sky.

9

The other day, a friend said to me, *They've opened the Christmas aisle.*
She said it with a grimace, but from me, it provoked a smile.

You see, I'm one of those annoying people who love this season,
And though I don't have to, I'll explain my reason:

To me, Christmas is all about the lights and the tree,
They're both powerful symbols of hope and growth, you see.

And it's not just Christians who celebrate at this time,
Loving to hear the church bells chime.

In Hanukkah's glow, Diwali's radiance, and Yule's embracing light,
Amid winter's harshness, lights twinkle, chasing away the night.

All faiths keep the light burning until the return of the sun.
I have to admit, though, I also find glitter and sparkle fun!

So, though I celebrate Christmas for reasons deep,
Following Dickens' advice, every day in my heart, its spirit I shall keep.

10

Today is Friday when folks like to dress down,
But why not don your finest gown,

Or best suit, just for a lark?
Yes, it might deliver that Friday spark.

'Cos when you make an effort, people take note,
And to winter's gloom, you'll be a living antidote.

For what you wear has an effect:
It can illustrate that you have self-respect.

So, make Friday fabulous with what you wear,
Stand out, rather than fit in—yes, show that you dare.

11

Today, I'm meeting a friend for drinks,
One of the greatest joys in life, methinks.

Through jovial banter, our worries wane,
And friendship's bond we thus maintain.

Each sip we take, a memory we send,
In the circle of trust, our joys transcend.

As we remember how we got together,
And affirm our promise to be pals forever.

We clink our glasses and say, *chin-chin*,
Staying positive, whatever state life's in.

To the cherished times without end;
The joy of drinking with my beloved friend.

12

On Strictly, last night, the judges held up their scores,
High for some, but others declared bores.

How hard must it be to be judged like this,
With everything noted that was amiss.

And though, in life, we may not aim for that Glitter Ball,
Be careful that for the judging game you don't fall.

Whether you're scoring others, or yourself, for what you do,
Kindness is the key that will see you through.

So, your friend is a *4* at organisation,
And your hubby's the untidiest in the nation,

But to you, their friendship and love score a *10*.
Now, look at yourself again.

Where in life do you excel?
Yes, look closely, and you'll deserve a *10* as well!

13
Today's truly is a Moon-day, for today the moon is new,
A brilliant start to the week for me and you.

For new moons are a great time to make a new start,
And to make a wish straight from the heart.

If you do, as the moon grows full in the sky,
Your dreams will come true if you try,

To set your goals and manifest.
For helping the dreamers is what the new moon does best.

14
This week is self-care week, celebrating a basic need, not a luxury.
If practised, you'll have energy for others; no greater gift could there be.

In the hustle of life, don't forget to be kind,
To yourself, dear friend, let go of the worries on your mind.

In the chaos around, take a moment to breathe,
Your mind is an ocean; try looking beneath.

Breathe in the calm, exhale the strife,
Nourish your soul, embrace this life.

A warm bath, a book, or a stroll in the park,
Self-love's an essential and brings light to the dark.

15

Hello dear friend, I'm just a little bee,
And though brightly coloured, you may not notice me.

But if you take a closer look, you'll find that I'm great,
For your food and flowers exist because I pollinate.

Sometimes I'm a drone, and sometimes I'm a queen,
Or a worker who looks after the kids and keeps our beehive clean.

If I spot a source of pollen, I'll do a little dance,
To tell friends in my hive that the spot is worth a chance.

I've got to end this rhyme with a fact that is quite sad:
Bees are dying out because we've lost the habitats we had.

So if I may make so bold as to submit a little plea:
Plant flowers, stop the chemicals: we need each other, you see.

16

Today, I have to wait for a tradesman's call,
Given a four-hour slot, inconvenient overall.

I could complain and feel quite blue,
Yet maybe there's something else I can pursue.

Instead of waiting, I'll use this time,
To catch up on a soap, or write a rhyme.

When he eventually does show,
I'll greet him with a cheery *Hello!*

Thanking him for a break from life's strife,
Helping me hit pause on my hectic life.

17
Without revealing my life's plot,
To me, what I'm called means a lot.

You see, to me, Sue belongs in my past,
While Susan is my present and future; quite a contrast.

People's names matter; they should be theirs to choose,
For they contain the shades of their world, a thousand hues.

18
We like to know a person's age,
It helps us put them in a social cage.

Truth is, though, no matter what the calendar says,
We're each of us many ages through our days.

When I dance, I'm vibrant, sexy 25;
75 is how I feel when into my tax form I must dive.

Giggling with a friend means I'm 17;
Heading out in my finery, a 35-year-old queen.

As I get excited hearing Christmas tunes,
I'm 5 again, loving rainbows and balloons.

So when we're out and about and meet on the street,
Let's not make assumptions about the age of those we greet.

For today, they may be feeling young and full of fun,
After all, age IS just a number, when all is said and done.

19

On Strictly, it was Tower Ballroom week,
When every couple dances their best to seek,

A *10* from every judge; applause from the crowd,
Reward for their efforts; the right to feel proud.

The couples tried hard to shine bright,
To rival the Illuminations in the Blackpool night.

Some danced boldly and seized the hour;
Others stood as tall as the iconic Tower.

Though, for some, the Glitter Ball seemed further out of reach,
And, for them, the night certainly was no walk on the beach.

Through the judges' feedback, they tried to smile,
Longing to be anywhere but on the Golden Mile.

For the Stars, this night was like The Big One,
A roller coaster ride of anxiety and fun.

20

I am a poet who loves to alliterate,
But you have to be careful, 'cause using it might berate,

The thing you are describing, take today—
Let's take a look at what we say:

Monday is often seen as a day of misery and pain,
Or, at the very most, of the humdrum and mundane.

So let's see what we can do to save Monday's rep,
How about Mirthful Monday that'll put a spring in our step?

Or let's treat this Monday as something to motivate:
A chance to set our week up for the great.

Finally, Miraculous Monday, a chance to go far,
Aim for the Moon and you might bag yourself a star.

21

Tuesdays, my friend, can seem a bit *blah*,
A day when the weekend seems so far.

It's not the hero of the week and doesn't have Friday delight,
But what if we look at it in a different light?

Let's turn Tuesday into *Choose Day*, then it's got its own vibe.
What are you gonna choose: a cosy night in, or a chance to imbibe?

A canvas for dreams; a slate yet unclaimed,
Opportunity whispers; delights unnamed.

So embrace Tuesday with its humble cheer,
For in its midst, treasures may appear.

22

If it's your birthday today, you're a Sagittarian,
You've an adventurous spirit filled with fun.

You're a fire sign filled with energy,
One of the friendliest folks there could be.

Outgoing and gregarious,
You have a talent for being hilarious.

Though wise and honest, you sometimes lack tact,
But you're fiercely loyal, and that's a fact.

You share your birthday sign with Taylor Swift and Brad Pitt,
You've a sunny nature and, with others, you'll always be a hit.

So dear Sagi, please enjoy your birthday time,
With your intelligence, you are sure to appreciate this little rhyme.

23

Do you know your neighbour's name?
Or, in aloofness, do you remain?

In the spaces where homes align,
You could create something fine.

A wave hello; a friendly smile,
Turns your house into a home, worthwhile.

To lend a hand; to spread some cheer;
Sharing news with those so near.

And any rifts that might arise,
With kindness, you can harmonize.

Being neighbourly makes your space so fair,
So say Hello to a neighbour today, go on, dare!

24

Yesterday, I took a journey – it wasn't long,
But, for a day, it helped my heart sing a different song.

Weighed down by the responsibilities of adult life,
For a day, I could forget the strife.

I went to see a friend and we talked of our dreams,
And how, in the midst of muck, a diamond always gleams.

With each other, a different viewpoint we could find,
A chance to open our hearts and expand the mind.

On paths that seem quite brief and small,
Lies the chance to learn from all.

Short journeys, though they may seem slight,
Hold treasures hidden in plain sight.

25

Winter winds have begun to blow;
It would be easy to start to feel quite low.

So here's a little trick you can use
To get the mindset that you choose:

Create a playlist of summer tunes,
Ones that remind you of balmy nights amidst sand dunes.

Why not give *California Girls* a play,
Or *Club Tropicana* to conjure up a lovely day?

It's up to you; you've only you to please,
But hot days could be conjured up with *Summer Breeze*.

Listen well, and soon you'll be feeling warm and fine,
And even in winter's darkest days, *Walking on Sunshine*.

26

A Hopi elder once said, *To watch us dance is to hear our hearts speak*,
So imagine the bravery it takes, week after week,

On Strictly, to expose yourself to the crowd,
To reveal your inner self, loud and proud.

So let's be careful when we watch the celebs dance,
And if we like them, or not, give kindness a chance.

For celebs they may be, but they all have hopes and fears,
Like us, they've endured laughter and tears.

Now to judgment, each week, they submit,
Let them inspire us in our own dance of life, not to quit.

But to be brave and keep on dancing through the pain,
For life's really about learning to dance in the rain.

27

Tonight's full moon, with its light so bright,
Is the *Mourning Moon*—a chance to shine light,

On what the heart still truly bears,
And cleanse your soul of life's heavy cares.

In the lunar glow, it's a time to grieve,
Embrace sorrows, yet still believe,

That once you've let things and people go,
Your New Year will bring joy, this I know.

This time of reflection I urge you to embrace,
Then the next full moon will find you in a better place.

28

Imagine that you had a magical device,
A remote control that governed your life precise.

Buttons and switches, a powerful hold,
Control at your fingertips, stories untold.

Pressing play, you set the day aglow,
With dreams to chase and places to go.

Fast forward through moments that you dread,
Pause the chaos that swirls in your head.

Rewind to cherish the joys of the past,
Skip the hurdles and make them vanish fast.

Volume down on doubts and fears,
Muting negativity and drying up tears.

Channelling energies, choices abound,
Switching directions with a simple sound.

A remote for life, a tool so grand,
In your grip, is Fate's command.

But amidst this control, a truth so clear,
Life's not a script, nor a show to steer.

For in spontaneity, life finds its thrill,
Remote or not, it's your heart's will.

So, while this remote grants some reprieve,
Life's joy lies in what we believe.

It's not just buttons, power, or might,
But living each moment and embracing the light.

29
I hadn't slept and had troubles galore,
How was I gonna get out the door?

I needed something to inspire,
A thought from someone I admire.

Regina Brett said, *No matter how you feel, get up, dress up, and show up*,
Maybe that thought could help fill my empty cup.

I'll try a bit of lippy to help rejuvenate,
And maybe some earrings to help me feel great.

Now out and about, I get the odd compliment,
From folks who, to me, were Heaven-sent.

Remember, no matter how you feel,
Love starts with you, that's the deal,

For in this life, we all suffer sorrow,
Sometimes bravery is saying, *I'll try again tomorrow*.

30
Each day when I wake, there's something I do,
Whether feeling chirpy, or quite blue.

I sit down with a coffee and my favourite soap,
And somehow, with life's trials, it helps me cope.

Yes, I cherish my morning routine,
For my day it sets the tone, like a well-tuned machine.

This ritual grounds me, granting a steady flow,
Amidst chaos, a familiar glow.

In times of change, my little habits hold me tight,
In moments of darkness, they shine bright.

They offer solace, a guiding light,
Through life's journey, day and night.

December

1

On Faux Fur Friday, hear the call,
Where fashion meets conscience for one and all.

Soft and cosy in coats without harm in their wake,
Embracing warmth, for ethics' sake.

Fur, not real, yet just as grand,
Adorning outfits, taking a stand.

No animals harmed in this attire,
Style and compassion, a perfect desire.

Faux Fur Friday, a trend that's bright,
Celebrating kindness, shining light.

Let's wear our choices, proud and true,
Compassion in fashion, for me and you!

In a world where kindness we pursue,
There's a magic phrase for me and you.

It's simple, yet profound, tried and true,
The phrase is *Thank You*, in all we do.

Gratitude blooms like a vibrant flower,
Brightening hearts in each passing hour.

It lifts the spirit, empowers the soul,
Making others feel truly whole.

For when we express our heartfelt praise,
We ignite joy in numerous ways.

It shows appreciation, sincere and pure,
A treasure that forever shall endure.

A thank you carries immense weight,
It melts away worries, anger, and hate.

It fosters bonds and strengthens ties,
Bringing warmth beneath the skies.

So let's cherish this humble art,
And Gratitude's song within our heart.

3

This week, on Strictly of Musicals, it was a celebration,
As, once again, the celebs tried to win the hearts of the nation.

The couples hoped that the judges' comments wouldn't be *Wicked*,
And that their performances wouldn't be insipid.

There were nerves aplenty, one could tell,
As each hoped to put on a show that was *Belle*.

A *Backstage Romance* had been noticed and discussed,
But that didn't matter and all seemed nonplussed.

Though there was a little *Dirty Dancing*,
To *Step in Time*, there was joyful prancing.

A fantastic show was put on by all,
Now, onwards and upwards, towards that Glitter Ball.

4

On team-building days, a common ice breaker over tea,
Is, *If you were an animal, what would you be?*

And the answers you hear can be quite revealing.
If someone answers, *A fly, so I can spy on folks from the ceiling*,

Or, *A sloth who spends the day in a dozy dream*,
Are these folks that you would want on your team?

What if someone says *A bear*?
That might bring to mind a hug, but then there are those who could tear,

You limb from limb, so next time you hear people's answers, take note.
Listen intently, like an intelligent stoat.

And as for me, what animal would I be?
A tropical fish living in a very warm sea.

Colourful and cute, they make people smile,
They help you forget your worries, just for a little while.

5

Carbon is amazing: it makes many things,
From a lump of coal to the diamonds in our rings.

Also made of carbon are me and you,
We can shine bright as gems, yet be gritty too.

In life's furnace, trials robust,
We're diamonds formed from coal's dark dust,

So the lesson of this little rhyme,
Is that within us lies both shine and grime.

So next time you see another, you must decide,
To keep your eyes open wide.

For even though they may lack lustre,
Your imagination you must muster.

For we all, like carbon, this special ore,
Hold brilliance deep within our core.

6

You've got a magic Advent Calendar, what are you wishing for?
Is it a bit of peace and quiet, or someone to adore?

Or to end a feud with a long lost friend?
Perhaps it is security, abundance without end?

As each day passes and doors swing wide,
Remember your dreams that linger inside.

For beyond the sweets and the festive cheer,
Lie the wishes of your heart; those things you hold dear.

Here's a thought: perhaps your own Secret Santa you could be,
Give your heart its Advent wish and fill your life with glee.

7

It's December, and as you begin to review your year,
Do you feel you deserve a boo, or cheer?

Has the year been a breeze and filled with fun,
Or has every victory been hard-won?

Well, as you conduct your review,
I urge you to give yourself credit where credit's due.

Try to look over the year with an Angel's eyes,
Have there been any blessings in disguise?

Life can be hard, but we must all stand tall,
For *The greatest glory in living lies not in never falling, but in rising every time we fall*

Quote by: Nelson Mandela

8

A little nail polish for me each day is a must,
And I love the names like *Arabesque* and *Stardust*.

In Winter, as *Tropical Sunset* I apply,
I'm transported to a cloudless sky.

When I look at my hands and see *Fuchsia Fun*,
I imagine that all my drudge is done.

There's even a polish called *Serendipity*,
Something nice, accidentally.

So if you need a lift, here's a trick that won't fail:
Apply a little colour to each nail.

For there's fun to be had in these pots of pleasure,
Champagne Shimmer will help us the little things to treasure.

9

In a world so fast, where moments quickly fade,
Sending Christmas cards, a tradition well-made.

Through paper and ink, our thoughts take flight,
Bringing warmth and joy in the silent night.

In these cards, emotions beautifully penned,
Connecting hearts, no matter the trend.

Across the miles, they bridge the space,
Spreading love and cheer, a familiar embrace.

A simple gesture, yet it holds such might,
Bringing smiles and hope, shining so bright.

In a digital age, where clicks swiftly dart,
A handwritten note touches the heart.

For in these cards, a tale is told,
Of friendship, love, and stories old.

They carry memories, both near and far,
Keeping traditions, like a guiding star.

For on that day the recipient may just need a little lift.
Each envelope may contain an unknown gift.

So, let's keep alive this heartfelt art,
Sending Christmas cards, a piece of heart.

10

Strictly's a show whose glitz and glamour we adore,
It has given us this season, though, so much more.

Teaching us how to develop self-belief,
And how to move forward through life despite the grief.

We've learnt that even if we don't win,
We triumph if we become comfortable in our own skin.

Now we can embrace being brave and bold,
Though the world may treat us as done and old.

Once you may have danced like a Dad,
Who cares? You're having the most fun you've ever had!

So though you're not a celeb, you can be a star.
Go out today, dance proud, and show the world who you are!

11

It's been announced that the word of the year is *Rizz*.
I rather like it, as it rhymes with fizz.

It's a lovely word that does no harm,
And expresses the qualities of charisma and charm.

Words that have in the past been given this accolade,
Include *Fake News*, in which all media outlets seem to trade.

Selfie has also made the list,
Doing one is something of which we've all had to get the gist.

But thankfully, not all of us have started to *Vape*,
So we get to choose whether to adopt a word or escape,

And create our own word of the year.
Of course, being the Cosmic Rhymer, mine's got to be *Stratosphere*.

12

Though the darkest of nights may invoke a sense of doom,
The new moon holds a promise to cast off the old gloom.

A celestial cue for us to start anew;
To approach with hope all that we pursue.

A beacon of hope, in its crescent embrace,
We're encouraged to hope and put fear in its place.

With an open heart, let our wishes flow,
As the future looks brighter with this cosmic show.

So let's revel in this lunar invitation,
Embrace the joy, the mirth, the elation.

new moon's allure, a reminder so clear,
That in our lives, if we look, the magic is always near.

13

Are you hoping for a Christmas that's white?
Well, though it may not snow, adding white to our lives can help us feel bright.

It can help hold us in a serene embrace,
Bringing calm and order to a festive, cluttered space.

Amidst a time of year that's *do, do, do*,
White will bring peace to me and you.

And as we look ahead to a fresh year,
It's good to keep white near.

For white is the colour of new starts,
A blank piece of paper on which we can scribe the wishes of our hearts.

14

I used to have a dumb phone, now I've gone Smart,
But that little phone will always have a place in my heart.

It was fuchsia pink, and it didn't do much,
Though I could fire off texts with a lightning touch.

I could archive messages, set reminders, it was all that I needed.
Please go smart, I can send you pics, my husband often pleaded.

I gave in when my little phone started to let me down,
The security codes I requested didn't arrive, which made me frown.

Messages I was sure that I had sent,
Somehow got lost within the ferment.

I marched into my provider's shop and said, *Swap my SIM,*
For a smartphone one. For the smirk he gave, I won't forgive him.

I am discovering, though, my smartphone has a benefit,
I choose emojis to attach and demonstrate my wit.

And though my texting's slower, something I find tough,
The greatest thing of all is now my ringtone is *Mr. Big Stuff*!

15

Some folks are fountains, sprouting light and cheer,
Their energy flows, spreading far and near.

They bubble with joy, their spirits in flight,
Refreshing all with their vibrant, bright, light.

Then there are others, akin to drains,
Sucking up energy; leaving few gains.

They siphon away, leaving hearts worn,
Draining the vigour; leaving souls torn.

Fountains uplift, with their positive stream,
While drains deplete, like a fading dream.

Choose to be a fountain, you might as well try,
Spreading joy and light as times go by.

For yesterday I met a fountain and she transformed my day,
What you do, and what you give, matters; choose carefully your way.

16

Have you ever thought that if you were to reincarnate,
Would you like to be an ordinary Joe, or some historical great?

I think I'd like to come back as a Hollywood film star,
Being driven around in a fancy car.

But then I might get hounded by the press,
And my lack of privacy might cause distress.

Okay, so, how about a castaway on a tropical isle?
Hmm, no TV, friends, or shopping trips to make me smile.

What about a sporting hero—but then I'd have to train?
Lack of chocolate and cocktails: such a pain.

No, if I come back, I think I'd best stick to being me,
Imperfect, quirky, but a greater rhymer there could never be!

17

The final of Strictly, nerves palpable,
There was already a winner, though; all could tell.

One for whom the night held no fear,
'Cause she's already had a dazzling career.

Yes, as Cher shone like a Christmas ornament,
Singing her heart out to our content.

The celebs danced but could not match this most special of divas,
Who, in the existence of Christmas Angels, made us all believers.

As the glitter ball for the finalists was in sight,
Christmas came early for all, thanks to Cher, Queen of this Christmas night.

18

It's that time of year when we are asked to give a thought to charity.
Ah, but there's a cost-of-living crisis; I hear your plea.

You're struggling to fund even your Christmas dinner.
You feel more like a loser than a festive winner.

No chance of buying an Elf on the Shelf?
Well, here's a thought: give of yourself.

For there are things you can do that won't cost a pound,
And in doing them, the true spirit of Christmas you will have found.

Speak to a lonely neighbour for a while,
That's bound to make Santa smile.

Volunteer an hour in a charity shop,
You'll find the joy and good vibes won't stop.

Please don't think that there's nothing you can do,
For someone, somewhere, today is in need of YOU.

Give yourself the gift of self-belief,
For it is in giving that we do receive.

19

In winter's grasp, when all seems bare,
Evergreen trees, resilient, they dare,

To stand unwavering, amidst the cold,
Their verdant hues, a tale they've told.

Symbol of constancy, through time they stand,
Their steadfast nature, across the land,

In snow-kissed woods, a timeless scene,
Their enduring presence, evergreen.

Amidst the frost, where winter bites;
The Christmas tree, cheering up long, cold nights,

Holly and mistletoe, adorning bright,
Emblems of love, hope and light.

With red and green, a vibrant blend,
Their significance: a message to send.

Evergreen trees, their boughs uplift,
A testament to life; an ageless gift,

When all seems dead with no life to see,
They offer us a glimpse of eternity.

20

Today is National Go Caroling Day,
A day to wrap up warm and go out of your way,

To spread some Christmas joy with song,
For these beloved tunes can help us feel that we belong.

Everyone has their favourite that brings them light,
Mine's *O Little Town of Bethlehem*; yours might be *Silent Night*.

Even if you're not a singer, belting out carols can spread Christmas cheer.
Your reward after you're done: retreat to a cosy pub for a festive beer.

21

Tomorrow is The Solstice, when the sun seems to stall,
But in the darkness, there is hope for all.

For though we have to endure this, the longest night,
The Sun's regaining its power so it can once more shine bright.

The shortest day sings of a cycle anew,
With each passing moment, the light breaks through.

A beacon of hope in the cold, wintry haze,
The Solstice reassures: soon we'll welcome once more the sun ablaze.

It teaches a lesson so profound:
Keep faith in the light, for soon it will radiate again, triumphant and unbound.

22

Happy Birthday, Capricorn, the Sun moves into your sign today,
You are born determined to work, not play.

Your ambition soars to the highest peak,
With strong discipline, never timid or meek.

Practical minds with wisdom vast,
Capricorns climb obstacles, with determination that will last.

You're a diligent worker with your goal in sight,
Reliable and responsible, day and night.

With a sense of humour, often wry,
Your wit shines through, never too shy.

Capricorns are loyal in friendship and love,
Your devotion's unwavering, like stars above.

But beneath your tough, resilient shell,
Lies a tender heart, a secret you will seldom tell.

Capricorns, like the goat that is the symbol of your sign,
Will climb mountains high, without moan or whine.

So here's to the Capricorns, steadfast and true,
With determination and strength in all that you do.

And here's a lovely thought to make you feel bolder:
Capricorns are the longest-lived signs, a gift to cherish as you grow older.

23

Let's go to a Panto, a place where we can dream.
The magic there will make our eyes gleam.

There's fun to be had in every way,
With stories and songs to brighten our day.

How wondrous, too, if the story came alive!
If we had a fairy godmother, oh, how we'd thrive!

With magic and wonder, she'd always be near,
To ward off the bad and bring good cheer.

When a villain arrived, someone would shout,
They're behind you!, and on their evil ways they'd be called out.

A panto can be a beacon of light,
To steer us away from what's wrong and toward the right.

Yes, Panto can be a tonic for the spirit for me and you,
And we all need that at the moment, *Oh yes, we do!*

24

'Twas the night before Christmas', and some longed for a house,
Given temporary accommodation, treated like a louse.

Nowhere to hang their stockings with care,
Not feeling festive, but life is not fair.

In one room, there were several beds,
Fear and loneliness were the thoughts in their heads.

Suddenly, from outside, there arose such a clatter,
Too scared to go out and see what was the matter.

For they knew that it couldn't be St. Nick,
But a dangerous drunk, being sick.

Santa may be employed tonight, but they could find no work,
Each dismissed by society as a shirker and jerk.

Forgotten, abandoned, out of mind, and out of sight,
Please, spare a thought for the lost ones on this Christmas Eve night.

25

I have a friend called Holly, and then there's Mr. Edmonds, Noel.
What time of year were they born, can you tell?

Of course, they were born at the most festive time of year.
I wonder if we followed the principle, what interesting names we'd hear.

Would we come across someone called Valentine?
Or Guy, as in Fawkes? Now, that would be fine.

Summer, a lovely name to evoke a gentle breeze.
Surely, no one would be called Pumpkin, that would be a tease.

If born in March or April, perhaps they'd be called Bunny.
Hmm, not sure they would find that funny.

So, if you have a child at a special time or date,
Take time before you name them, for it's a forever label you allocate!

26

Boxing Day has arrived, it's time to be,
Watching sporting events, or on a shopping spree.

Deals galore; a merry dance;
Hustle, bustle; a shopping trance.

In homes, TV screens glow bright,
Sports fans gather, hoping the result will be right,

Cheering loud for their team's play,
On this festive sporting day.

Or maybe you're just having a rest,
Congratulating yourself because this Christmas was the best.

You're having a break from being Santa's chief elf,
Go on, choose yourself a pressie from that shelf.

27

What's your favourite work of art?
Mine's *The Scream*, that gives you a glimpse into my heart.

Now maybe Banksy's more your thing,
And *Girl with a Balloon* makes your heart sing.

Dad was a miner, working deep in the ground,
In Constable's *The Haywain* countryside bliss he found.

Art can help us express or transport,
Us to higher realms when life seems fraught.

So from Van Gogh to Hockney and Claude Monet,
Let's hear it for the artists, opening up vistas, showing us the way.

28

What's your view on Philosophy?
Do you roll your eyes and say, *It's all Greek to me*?

Here's a secret I'd like to impart:
Ancient Greek philosophy has wisdom for your head and heart.

Socrates taught that in life it's not what happens to you;
But much more about how you choose to view,

Events in your life, be they good or bad:
If you alter your thinking, in your soul, you can still be glad.

Aristotle argued for everything in moderation,
A concept now familiar throughout our nation.

He taught that a balanced life was a happy one,
And to do good when it needed to be done.

If you find yourself in a tight spot,
Ancient philosophy could help you a lot.

29

In this world, a dance, a cosmic play,
Five elements weave through night and day.

Within us, they form our very core,
In balance, our lives align and soar.

Have you felt the joy of walking on air,
Or flowed like water without a care?

At times as sturdy as rooted wood,
A sense of security deeply understood.

Perhaps your inner fire brightly burns,
A dazzling sight at every turn.

Then, strong as metal, a conduit's might,
These elements blend, pure and right.

A symphony within, in perfect guise,
Nature's canvas, where beauty lies.

In and out, balance is the key,
A dance of existence, in you and me.

30

I love lists, for me a sense of order they do install,
They guide me forward in life when I hit a wall.

Line by line, they come alive,
Goals and hopes, they make me thrive.

A catalogue of what to do,
Organized steps to see me through.

In checkboxes lies a world of glee,
Ticking off what's meant to be.

Each item marked, a little win,
Bringing joy from deep within.

So here's to lists, big or small,
Things to Do, or life-plan, I love them all.

There's one list though above all that I adore,
A daily note of all the things in life I'm grateful for!

31

Tonight, midwinter, resolutions will bloom,
Yet nature whispers a different tune.

When frosty winds, their bite impart,
Is that the time for a fresh start?

Spring's vibrant hues, they beckon near,
Nature's pulse, alive and clear.

Bathed by the sun, nurtured and warm,
Is where ambitions find their form.

As buds unfurl, so does the mind,
In sync with nature, aligned and kind.

The energy of growth, it surges high,
Supports aspirations to reach the sky.

Winter's grip, is harsh and cold:
Not the time for dreams to unfold.

But spring, O spring, is nature's cue,
To nurture goals, both old and new.

So let the seasons guide your way,
For resolutions, wait for spring's empowering day.

Thank you for joining me on this poetic journey through A Year of Rhyme, crafted with heart and a touch of cosmic sparkle.

I hope my work has brought you joy, reflection, and perhaps a smile on an ordinary day.

For inquiries regarding publication, interviews, and speaking engagements, please reach out to me at safinnerty@yahoo.co.uk

With gratitude,

Susan Armstrong-Finnerty
The Cosmic Rhymer